The History of Science Fiction

The History of Science Fiction

by Ron Miller

Franklin Watts
A Division of Scholastic Inc.
New York / Toronto / London / Auckland / Sydney
Mexico City / New Delhi / Hong Kong
Danbury, Connecticut

This book is very gratefully
dedicated to Bob Burns.

Much appreciation is due to David A. Kyle, Sam Moskowitz,

James Gunn, Bob Burns, and Pamela Sargent.

Cover illustration by: Vincent Di Fate
Frontis: ©Frank Kelly Freas
Interior design: Molly Heron

Photographs ©: AKG London: 12, 18 top; AP/Wide World Photos: 49 (Fiona Hanson); Archive Photos: 96 (Fotos International), 126 (Scott Sutton), 99, 105; Bridgeman Art Library International Ltd., London/New York: 18 bottom (BEN 100347/ Galleria degli Uffizi, Florence, Italy), 90 (JF 131244/ Private Collection); Everett Collection, Inc.: 9, 106, 74; Frank Kelly Freas: 2, 41; James Gurney/BDSP: 62, 63; Mary Evans Picture Library: 21, 23, 28, 31, 35, 39, 71, 76, 94, 111, 113, 115; Ron Miller (author): 53, 58, 61, 79; Photofest: 99 inset, 101, 108; Smithsonian Institution, Washington, D.C.: 78, 117; Stephen Hickman: 85; Wayne Barlow: 119.

Library of Congress Cataloging-in-Publication Data

Miller, Ron, 1947-
      The history of science fiction / Ron Miller
      p.cm.
      Includes bibliographical references and index.
      ISBN 0-531-11866-5 (lib. bdg.) 0-531-13979-4 (pbk.)
1. Science fiction—History and criticism—Juvenile Literature. [1. Science fiction—History and criticism.]
I. Title.

P96.S34 M55 2001
809.3'8762—dc21   00-036823

CONTENTS

"SF's no good," they bellow till we're deaf.
"But this looks good."—"Well, then, it's not SF."
      —Kingsley Amis/Robert Conquest

Chapter One
What Is Science Fiction?

The most difficult thing in talking about science fiction is defining exactly what science fiction is. There is no one quality that sets science fiction apart from any other kind of literature. Unlike a Western novel, for example, which is almost wholly defined by the location of its action, a science fiction novel has no readily identifiable setting. Nor does science fiction have any kind of action special to it, such as detective stories do. Science fiction is defined more by its ideas. As science fiction author Frederik Pohl said, science fiction is "a characteristic way of thinking about things."

There have been as many different definitions as people who make them. John W. Campbell Jr., the editor of *Astounding,* one of the first science fiction magazines, said that science fiction "consists of the hopes and dreams and fears (for some the dreams are nightmares) of a technically based society." Groff Conklin, one of science fiction's most knowledgeable anthologists, suggested that science fiction was "composed of 'supernatural' writing for materialists. You may read every science fiction story that is true science fiction, and never once have to compromise with your id. The stories all have rational explanations, provided you are willing to grant the word 'rational' a certain elasticity." The famous science fiction author Isaac Asimov defined "social science fiction [as] that branch of literature which is concerned with the impact of scientific advance upon human beings." "A [good] science fiction story," wrote Theodore Sturgeon in one of the best definitions of all, "is a story built around human beings, with a human problem and a human solution, which would not have happened at all without its scientific content."

There has always been a need to separate science fiction from outright fantasy—such as the ghost story, fairy tale, or tales of witchcraft and magic—and many definitions attempt to do this. It's a difficult task since the line between fantasy and science fiction is not clearly drawn, especially since science fiction's roots lay in fantasy. Author and historian David Kyle pointed out that "science fiction is fantasy fiction written under the strict new rules of science. Thus, though science fiction is fantasy fiction, the inverse is not true." Sam Moskowitz, a historian and biographer of science fiction, said that science fiction "is a branch of fantasy identifiable by the fact that it eases the 'willing suspension of disbelief' on the part of its readers by utilizing an atmosphere of scientific credibility for its imaginative speculations in physical science, time, social science, and philosophy." Author and critic Kingsley Amis suggested that "science fiction is that class of prose narrative treating a situation that could not arise in the world we know, but which is hypothesized on the basis of some innovation in science or technology,

An illustration by Robert McCall for the movie *2001: A Space Odyssey*

or pseudo-science or pseudo-technology. It is distinguished from pure fantasy by its need to achieve verisimilitude and win the 'willing suspension of disbelief' through scientific plausibility." Editor Bruce Franklin said that most genres of fiction were just different attempts at describing reality, ". . . [r]ealistic fiction tries to imitate actualities, historical fiction past probabilities, science fiction possibilities, fantasy impossibilities." Editor Sam Merwin Jr. was more succinct: "Science fiction is fantasy wearing a tight girdle."

Still, no matter how carefully anyone's definition of science fiction is worded, it is never difficult to find at least one major exception. For every attempt to separate science fiction from fantasy, there is a science fiction ghost story or science fiction novel about wizards and dragons and magic, in which all of the fantasy elements have a scientific basis. There have even been science fiction detective stories, science fiction Westerns, and science fiction romances. A kind of halfway category has been invented to describe stories that seem to fall somewhere between science fiction and fantasy. They are called *science fantasy*, of course.

It has also been suggested by some that science fiction would better be called *speculative fiction*. With less emphasis on "hard science," it opens up the possibility of safely including the borderline cases. Unfortunately, the broader a definition gets, the less meaningful it is.

But accumulating definitions for every exception is no real answer, either. Perhaps the most useful definition, and perhaps the only one that actually has any hope of working, is the not-quite-tongue-in-cheek one once proposed by science fiction author Damon Knight: "Science fiction is that thing I'm pointing at when I say 'that's science fiction.'"

Although, as we will see, science fiction was invented nearly two hundred years ago, it is really a product of the twentieth century, a result of the incredible revolutions that have taken place in science and technology and the powerful role they have had in shaping our society. In the three hundred years between the seventeenth century and the nineteenth century only 191 books of "futuristic fiction" were published. Between 1900 and 1950 there were 510. Today, one out of every four or five books of fiction being published is science fiction or fantasy—1,500 to 2,000 titles every year.

How Science Fiction Got Its Name

Like its elusive definition, nothing about science fiction comes easily. Even the story of how it got its name is not a simple one.

Science fiction was not always called "science fiction." Until the early part of the twentieth century, no one knew quite *what* to call it. The publisher of the books by Jules Verne, author of the classic *20,000 Leagues Under the Sea*, originally called these books "extraordinary voyages," which was a very good definition since most of Verne's books did indeed describe some sort of fantastic journey or voyage. In England and the United States, such stories were called "scientific romances." In the nineteenth century, the word *romance*, when applied to literature, meant something very different from its current definition. A "romantic" novel usually dealt with stories of fantastic adventures or faraway places. One magazine tried out "invention stories," but fortunately it never caught on. Among all the variations, "scientific romance" remained the name of choice and lasted well into the 1930s. However, as more and more science fiction stories were published at the end of the nineteenth and the beginning of the twentieth centuries, "scientific romance" became inadequate—partly because it sounded old-fashioned and partly because the word *romance* had attached itself almost exclusively to love stories.

Every magazine publishing science fiction tried its hand at coming

Captain Nemo determines the position of the "Nautilus" with a sextant from the first edition of Jules Verne's *20,000 Leagues Under the Sea*.

up with a name for this peculiar form of literature. "Off-trail stories," "impossible stories," "scientific stories," "pseudo-scientific stories," "different stories," and the truly awful "weird-scientific stories" were all considered with varying degrees of success, but none ever quite caught on. In the 1920s, the editor and publisher of a series of magazines devoted to science, radio, and inventions—an immigrant from Luxembourg named Hugo Gernsback—began running one or two science fiction stories in each issue. He called these stories "scientific fiction." When Gernsback, inspired by the popularity of these stories, decided to publish a magazine devoted entirely to science fiction, he came up with the name *scientifiction* for them. (Gernsback loved inventing complicated new words like that. In one of his own science fiction stories, he came up with names like *phonotelephote,* for television, *hypnobioscope, detectophone, teleradiograph, scientificafé,* and *telemotorcoasters.*) Then, in 1929, he came up with the term *science fiction,* and it appeared in print in May of that year for the very first time.*

What Science Fiction Is About

There are almost as many different types of science fiction as there are authors writing it. The type of science fiction that most people think of when they use the word is what is known as "hard science fiction." This is science fiction that is based on a very realistic, accurate use of science, with science usually being the core and sometimes the very reason for the story. Jules Verne was a practitioner of hard science fiction as are authors Hal Clement, Arthur C. Clarke, and Larry Niven. Hard science fiction is the type that appeals most to the serious science

---

* Science fiction is usually referred to as "SF" by its fans, who concurrently consider the term sci-fi as something used only by non-SF readers and Hollywood.

fiction reader and fan. "Adventure science fiction," another type, is less interested in scientific or technological themes than it is in using science as the background for an exciting adventure—much in the same way that Westerns use the American West merely as a background or setting for their story. Adventure science fiction is by far the easiest kind to write and read and has always been the most popular. *New Wave* was a "soft" science fiction introduced in the 1950s and 60s. It exhibited much more interest in the psychological, humanistic, sociological, and political aspects of the *effects* of science on people and society as opposed to science for its own sake. In many ways it reflected the same social unrest and concerns that produced the beatniks and hippies. *Cyberpunk*, the newest variety, is an offshoot of hard science fiction; it deals with the high-tech world of cyberspace, but in its political awareness and psychological twists, it has roots in new wave science fiction. Since much of cyberpunk's success depends on its ability to shock, there is a limit it must eventually reach; it will either evolve into something new, or be replaced by something as different as it once was. In science fantasy there is less interest in "real" science. The author will often make up the science as he or she goes along, with no attempt at accuracy or realism. Very often in these stories, the "science" is thinly veiled magic. *Star Wars,* for example, is much more science fantasy than science fiction. Almost all of these categories can contribute to "literary science fiction," which endeavors to measure itself against traditional standards and values of fiction. This is the sort of science fiction that is most likely to be noticed by critics and librarians. Very often, however, since it is the kind of science fiction that is written by mainstream authors who want to try their hand in the field, it is better literature than it is good science fiction.

The "science" in science fiction does not have to be any of the obvious sciences, such as astronomy, physics, or scientific inventions such as robots or time machines. Just about any and everything that can be called a "science" has been the subject of a science fiction story at one time or another. There have been science fiction stories about mathematics, psychology, biology, botany, genetics, philosophy, sociology, anthropology, meteorology, medicine . . . and even subjects that no one would ever confuse with science, such as history, art, and religion.

Chapter Two
The Archaeology of Science Fiction

As modern as it might seem, science fiction is one of the very oldest types of literature. Depending on how loosely you care to define it, science fiction was written as long ago as A.D. 160. But most of these were little more than wild adventure stories, tall tales, and folklore; if someone journeyed to the moon, it was by magic or other supernatural means. The first author to describe a journey into space was Lukian. In his book *True History,* whose hero is carried to the moon by a whirlwind, he describes the Earth as it might look from the moon:

". . . we were suddenly caught up by a whirlwind, which turned our vessel several times around in a circle with tremendous speed and lift-

ed it more than three thousand stadia into the air, not setting it down again on the sea, but kept it suspended above the water at that height, and carried us on, with swelled sails, above the clouds. After an aerial voyage of seven days and seven nights, we sighted land in the air. It was an island, luminous, spherical and shining with strong light. We put into it, and having cast our anchor, landed. On examining the country, we discovered that was inhabited and cultivated. In the daylight we could see nothing from where we were, but when night came, other islands became visible to us in the surrounding air. Some close by, some larger and some smaller, with the appearance of fire. There was also another land below us, with cities, rivers, seas, woods and mountains on it. This, we concluded, was our own world . . ."

There could be no true science fiction before there was science, and there was very little science before the Renaissance brought the world out of a thousand-year-long dark age of ignorance and superstition.

The seventeenth century was the perfect time for the birth of science fiction. Not only was science free to study the world and universe we lived in, but more importantly scientists were free to openly share their discoveries.

One of the products of this new interest in science was the telescope, which was invented in the Netherlands in 1608. An Italian scientist named Galileo Galilei built one the very next year and turned it toward the heavens. Until then, no one thought of the moon and planets as *places*. In fact, the word *planet* originally didn't mean at all what it eventually came to mean to us: a world circling the sun, like the Earth does. In Galileo's time the word *planet* was still defined in Greek as "wanderer" because people thought the planets were nothing more than a special class of star that wandered through the night sky. There was

Galileo Galilei used his own telescopes to discover that the moon and planets were actually other worlds.

TVBVM OPTICVM VIDES GALILAEII INVENTVM, ET OPVS, QVO SOLIS MACVLAS
ET EXTIMOS IVNAE MONTES, ET IOVIS SATELLITES, ET NOVAM QVASI
RERVM VNIVERSITATE PRIMVS DISPEXIT A. MDCIX.

nothing else unusual or special about them. Certainly no one ever suspected that those little specks of light might be worlds like Earth. Almost as soon as Galileo announced his astonishing discovery that the moon and planets were in fact other worlds, many stories began to appear, describing journeys to them and the kind of life that might exist there. Some of this enthusiasm was inspired by the fact that at the same time, Sir Walter Raleigh and other explorers were discovering new worlds on Earth. Thousands of explorers, adventurers, colonists, and missionaries were making the journey to these unknown lands. Some people reasoned that if it were possible to explore the Earth's new worlds, which one can't even see from Europe, it would surely be possible to explore the new worlds in the sky, which anyone can look at during the night with their own eyes.

The first book to realistically speculate about a journey into space was written by one of Galileo's fellow astronomers, a German named Johannes Kepler (1571–1630). Published in 1634, after Kepler's death, *Somnium* describes a trip to the moon. Although the method of getting there was not very scientific (the hero is taken there by means of witchcraft), Kepler's descriptions of the conditions beyond the Earth's atmosphere and of what the surface of the moon might be like were strictly according to Galileo's discoveries. Even the life that is discovered on the moon is described according to the harsh visual conditions that exist on the lunar surface.

The first story about a trip to the moon published in English was Bishop Francis Godwin's much more fanciful *The Man in the Moone* (1638), in which the hero is carried to the moon by a team of swanlike birds called ganzas. Perhaps the strangest method of space travel was in David Russen's book *Iter Lunaire* (1703), where the hero is launched to the moon by means of a giant spring!

Between the sixteenth and the eighteenth centuries, there were many stories written about traveling into space, but few were realistic. The authors were usually much more interested in satire or humor and couldn't have cared less whether their descriptions of the moon and the planets or how their heroes got there were realistic or not. Still, for all of their lack of real science, the stories reflected the increasing fascination the public had about the possibility of traveling to other worlds and what might be found there. One French author, Cyrano de Bergerac, actually managed to hit upon the idea of using rockets to launch his hero into space in his book *Le Voyage dans la Lune* (1657). But he only gets half credit for doing so because he was trying to come up with the silliest ideas he could think of! For example, de Bergerac suggested that he might be able to fly to the moon by attaching bottles filled with dew to his body—after all, everyone knew that the sun caused dew to rise into the air!

The Inventors of Science Fiction

At the same time that science was making such great progress, so were inventors, as might be expected. There were hundreds of inventions, including the printing press, the electrical generator, the knitting machine, the steam engine, and scientific instruments such as the microscope, thermometer, and barometer. In 1783 an invention was made that changed science fiction forever: the balloon. First flown in France by the Montgolfier brothers, the balloon showed that people could leave the Earth by mechanical means. For the first time in history, human beings traveled farther away from the Earth than they could jump. To fiction writers this meant that a trip to the moon might not be such a fantastic idea. After all, they asked, what is the difference between traveling a few thousand feet into the sky and a journey of a

Edgar Allan Poe

quarter of a million miles, other than a mere matter of degree? Surely if science and technology could do one, they could do the other.

One of the first authors to take advantage of this progress was the American writer Edgar Allan Poe (1809–1849), and in the process he invented modern science fiction. In addition, he invented the short story, something else that proved to be very important to the evolution of science fiction. Like many others who had written space travel stories in the thirty or forty years after the Montgolfier's invention, Poe used a balloon to get his hero to the moon. But what set his space travel story "Hans Phaall—A Tale" (1835), apart from all the rest was the invention of verisimilitude. The word *verisimilitude* means "resembling truth" and is a technique by which facts of all kinds—real or imagined—are used to make an implausible or impossible idea sound believable. Poe wasn't content to merely say, as other authors had done before him, that his hero simply got into a balloon and took off for the moon. Instead, he described in detail how the balloon was built, what sort of gas it used, how it was launched, and the special arrangements that had to be made so its passenger could withstand the rigors of traveling in space. In other words, Poe did not ignore what science knew about the moon and the conditions beyond the Earth's atmosphere as other authors had done; he took these facts into account and used them to make his story even more realistic and believable. With Poe, science fiction took a big step out of the realm of sheer fantasy.

Throughout his brief life, Poe was fascinated by science, the future of science and—what makes him the direct ancestor of the modern science fiction author—the effects of science on society. He realized that these effects might not necessarily be good ones, as in one of his stories ("The Colloquy of Monos and Una") where he described a future in which " . . . huge smoking cities arose, innumerable. Green leaves shrank before the hot breath of furnaces. The fair face of Nature was deformed as with the ravages of some loathesome disease . . ."

Even Poe's horror tales are more the horror of science fiction than of the supernatural, which, in spite of his reputation, almost never

An illustration by Harry Clarke (1919) for Poe's story "The Colloquy of Monos and Una."

makes an appearance in his stories. The terrors experienced by his characters are terrors produced by their own minds, by their fears, anxieties, and guilts. In much of Poe's science fiction, the science involved was the subtle science of the human mind—psychology.

Not everyone, however, was as enamored with science as was Poe. Some authors saw a much darker side to progress. Earlier in the nineteenth century, an eighteen-year-old girl named Mary Wollstonecraft Shelley agreed to a dare that she couldn't write a more frightening story than her friends. The result was a novel about a scientist whose attempt to create artificial life ends in tragedy. *Frankenstein,* which was first published in 1818, was an immediate success. Herman Melville, William Dean Howells, and Nathaniel Hawthorne were among the many notable American authors who also tried their hand at science fiction, often with the same darker side as *Frankenstein.*

Perhaps the first writer anywhere to specialize in this new type of fiction was a young Irish immigrant named Fitz-James O'Brien. The most famous of his many stories is "The Diamond Lens" (1858), in which an inventor creates a super-microscope that allows him to discover an incredible world in a single drop of water:

> *"On every side I beheld beautiful organic forms, of unknown texture, and colored with the most enchanting hues . . . While I was speculating on the singular arrangements of the internal economy of Nature, with which she so frequently splinters into atoms our most compact theories, I thought I beheld a form moving slowly through the glades of one of the prismatic forests . . . It was a female human shape . . . I cannot, I dare not, attempt to inventory the charms of this divine revelation of perfect beauty. Those eyes of mystic violet, dewy and serene, evade my words. Her long, lustrous hair following her glorious head in a golden wake, like the track*

sown in heaven by a falling star, seems to quench my most burning phrases with its splendors . . ."

The inventor falls in love with the microscopic girl, but he eventually loses her when the drop evaporates.

If science fiction had been invented by Poe, it was perfected and made popular by Jules Verne (1828–1905). Trained in law and working unhappily as a stockbroker in Paris, young Verne yearned for a literary life but had great difficulty in selling the plays and short stories he wrote. Finally, he tried his hand at a long nonfiction book about the possible use of balloons in African exploration. This was rejected, too, and he was about to throw the manuscript into the fire when his wife urged him to try just one more publisher. This time the book was accepted—but with one condition: that Verne rewrite it as a novel. He did so and the result, *Five Weeks in a Balloon* (1863), became a bestseller. He followed up this success with *A Journey to the Center of the Earth* (1864) and *From the Earth to the Moon* (1865). He ultimately wrote some sixty-six books and novels that took his readers to literally every corner of the world.

Edgar Allan Poe was one of Verne's favorite authors. From Poe he learned the technique of verisimilitude. Verne invented things that were always based on actual science and technology, and what Verne created always seemed perfectly possible. In *From the Earth to the Moon,* he described exactly how the cannon was built and the materials used. He explained every detail of the projectile that would carry the passengers to the moon and meticulously listed every one of the supplies they were taking along.

Verne even provided his readers with the mathematical calculations on which the whole project was based. So realistic, in fact, were the descriptions in this book that when the novel was originally serialized, hundreds of people wrote to the magazine volunteering to be passengers on the first trip!

Although Verne is famous for his fantastic inventions, such as the fabulous submarine *Nautilus* in *20,000 Leagues Under the Sea* (1870), his real fascination with creating them was to enable his heroes to travel to places where no other person had gone before. The projectile in *From the Earth to the Moon,* for example, gave his characters and readers an eyewitness look at the moon; and the *Nautilus* allowed Verne to take his readers into the depths of the ocean and introduce them to the then-new science of oceanography.

But Verne's books are not just about amazing inventions and strange places. He was also interested in the effects of science and technology on people. Using these effects enabled him to examine the human condition, which is what makes science fiction so valuable. Verne was a political liberal and used his books to expound upon his deeply felt ideas concerning liberty and individualism. Where so many other Victorian authors—such as Rudyard Kipling—championed conquest and imperialism, Verne steadfastly opposed it. Many of his most heroic characters, such as Captain Nemo, are self-sufficient rebels or voluntary outcasts from society. Nemo, for example, spends much of his time gathering sunken treasure that he uses to finance revolutions against tyrannical governments. "Music, freedom, and the sea" were Verne's three great loves, and they also describe what his heroes most loved, too.

Verne's work was a perfect mirror of the public's idolization of the engineer and explorer. His books are a celebration of progress. However, writing as he did for nearly forty years, his work also reflects how the public felt as the nineteenth century drew to a close: scientists and engineers were just as capable of destroying life as making it better. Even the United States—a country he loved and admired and the setting for more than a third of his novels—takes on an ever darker cast toward the end of Verne's career. The last of Verne's novels became increasingly pessimistic about the possibility of science used to improve mankind's lot. A perfect example of this is seen by comparing two of his novels, *Robur the Conqueror* (1886) and *The Master of the World* (1904), the sequel to *Robur*, which was published the year before Verne died. In the first book, Robur is an heroic champion of the glorious future of aviation who invents a super-helicopter that he uses to explore the world. But when he returns in the sequel, it is in the role of a madman, bent on using his knowledge solely for world conquest. The scientist-hero had become the scientist-destroyer.

Verne's career overlapped with that of his successor, British writer H.G. Wells (1866-1946), who had begun publishing short stories and essays in the 1890s. Wells's work was popular, but with the publication of the short novel *The Time Machine* in 1895, when he was not quite thirty years old, he became world famous. The story also heralded a major change in direction for science fiction.

The Time Machine was very much a product of the end of the nineteenth century, focusing on the disillusionment of science and imperialism as well as deep concern for social issues. In the far distant future of the year A.D. 802,701, the Time Traveler discovers a world where the gentle, peaceful Eloi are literally raised as fodder for the degenerate, subterranean, cannibalistic Morlocks. This was how Wells saw his own world, with its working people becoming ever more the victims of a seemingly out-of-control industrial class. "Machinery," Wells wrote later about these two levels of society, "has made them into different species . . ." In *The Time Machine,* this becomes literally true.

The TIME MACHINE
~ By H.G. Wells ~

Author of "The First Men in the Moon," "The New Accelerator," etc.

An illustration by Frank R. Paul for Wells's *The Time Machine,* when it appeared in *Amazing Stories* in May 1927.

Wells followed the success of *The Time Machine* with *The Island of Dr. Moreau* (1896), *The Invisible Man* (1897), *The War of the Worlds* (1898), *First Men in the Moon* (1901), and dozens of other novels and scores of short stories. Almost all of these are still in print and just as readable today as they were a century ago.

In almost all his fiction, Wells uses science fiction as a kind of instrument—like a microscope or telescope—through which the social condition of humankind can be scrutinized more clearly than any other way. Just as in *The Time Machine,* where he described a two-class society carried to its ultimate extreme, *The War of the Worlds* showed Wells's Victorian readers a disturbing vision of what it might be like to be the conquered race instead of the conquering.

Other Contributors

At the end of the nineteenth century, a number of remarkable science fiction novels appeared, and all of them were quite different from one another. Many of their authors were drawn to the science fiction form because, similar to Verne and Wells, science fiction allowed them to more easily and explicitly explore the many social, philosophical, and psychological issues that concerned them. Even the multimillionaire John Jacob Astor—who had made his fortune in the fur trade—tried his hand at it, producing the interplanetary novel *On Other Worlds* (1899). Although its vision of the world in the twenty-first century is amazingly prophetic, Astor was embarrassed to have written such a book because it seemed beneath his place within New York society. Therefore, he tried to recall all of the copies and have them destroyed. A much more serious book was *Dr. Jekyll and Mr. Hyde* (1886), written by Robert Louis Stevenson, the author of *Treasure Island*. It is the story of a kindly doctor who discovers a drug that releases, for a short time, the dark, bestial side of his nature. Unfortunately, the drug is habit-forming. Finally, the evil side takes over completely and what results is tragic. In a sense, Stevenson took the doctor and the monster from *Frankenstein* and combined them into a single being. Today, *Dr. Jekyll and Mr. Hyde* has a great deal to say about the dual nature we all possess and the difficulty of keeping the two in balance. As in all good science fiction, Stevenson used science to explore some special quality about human beings that no other type of fiction could have done effectively.

Arthur Conan Doyle, creator of Sherlock Holmes, wrote several science fiction stories. Perhaps the best and most famous is *The Lost World* (1912), the exciting tale of the discovery of living dinosaurs on a remote plateau in South America. Even the British novelist and poet Rudyard Kipling, most famous for his stories about colonial India, such as *Kim* and *The Jungle Book,* tried his hand with two science fiction tales. In *With the Night Mail* (1905) and its sequel, *As Easy As A.B.C.* (1912), Kipling describes a future where commercial air transport companies (today we call them airlines) control the world.

Mark Twain may have invented the science fiction time travel story in his comic novel *A Connecticut Yankee in King Arthur's Court* (1889). His all-American hero, sent to the time of King Arthur by a lightning bolt, causes havoc by introducing such nineteenth-century innovations as pistols, bicycles, and newspapers. Another famous American author who tried his hand at science fiction was Edward Everett Hale, who is best known for his story, "Man Without a Country" (1863). When he wrote *The Brick Moon* (1869), he became the first person in history to suggest the possibility of an artificial Earth satellite. The Brick Moon is a two-hundred-foot-diameter hollow sphere made of brick to be launched into an orbit around the Earth where it would serve as a navigational aid for ships (exactly as satellites were to be used in the twentieth century). Unfortunately, it is accidentally launched with its work-men and their families still onboard. Most of the book deals with their efforts to stay alive on the new sphere.

Most American teenagers at the end of the nineteenth century got their science fiction in the form of the *dime novel* adventures. These sto-ries were hurriedly and often carelessly written, printed on the cheapest paper available, and in spite of their nickname actually cost only a nick-el. Literally hundreds were published, such as *The Steam Man of the Prairies, Frank Reade Jr. and His Electric Boat,* or *Frank Reade Jr.*

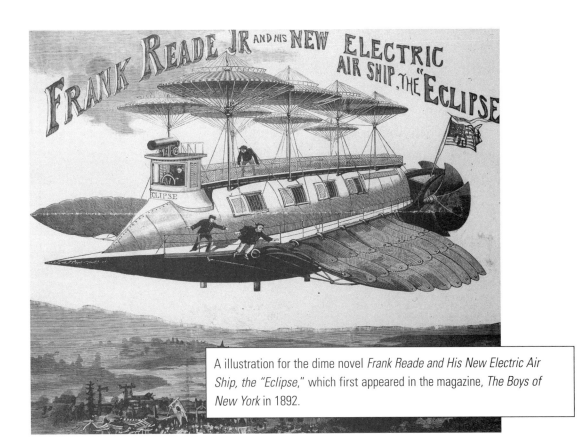

A illustration for the dime novel *Frank Reade and His New Electric Air Ship, the "Eclipse,"* which first appeared in the magazine, *The Boys of New York* in 1892.

and his Catamaran of the Air. The most popular series, those about young super-inventor Frank Reade Jr., were written by Lu Senarens. In his lifetime, Senarens may have published more than fifteen hundred dime novels under twenty-seven different pen names! Heavily influenced by—and even in some cases virtually copied from—Jules Verne,* Senarens's dime novels introduced an entire generation to the potential wonders of science and technology. However, at the same time they attached a stigma of cheapness, sensationalism, and immaturity to the name *science fiction*.

By the beginning of the twentieth century, the foundations for science fiction had been laid. All the pieces where there: the influence of real science, technology, discovery and invention; the use of verisimilitude and the creation of a sense of wonder in the reader; the establishment of the major themes, such as time and space travel, artificial life, utopias, supermachines, etc.; and, finally, the ideas of illustrating the impact of science on society and individual human beings, as well as the use of science fiction to illustrate social and psychological themes. Now all that was needed was a way to combine all of these into a distinctly new form of literature.

---

* Ironically, Senarens was often referred to as "the American Jules Verne," and there is even some evidence that he corresponded with the famous French author, who probably had little idea that he was not only being admired but blatantly copied.

The Birth of Science Fiction

A New Kind of Literature

A book was published in 1895 that forever changed how we looked at the other worlds we share with the solar system: Percival Lowell's *Mars* (1895). Lowell was a Bostonian amateur astronomer who had been wealthy enough to afford his own observatory in Arizona. From there he had "discovered" that the planet Mars was covered with a network of canals, and wrote of this discovery in *Mars* and in another book, *Mars and Its Canals* (1906). In them, he described a Mars that was a dying world, covered with dried-up seabeds and criss-crossed by huge canals carrying water from the poles to the arid deserts. He strongly believed in the existence of an ancient race of Martians who struggled desperately to survive. Although most other astronomers failed to see Lowell's canals and didn't believe they existed or even could exist,* Lowell's public believed in them. The whole idea of an ancient race battling against extinction appealed to the romantic Victorian mind, and most nonscientists believed that Lowell had proven that life had once existed on Mars—and maybe still existed. The idea that Mars might have "canals" lasted until 1965, when the NASA spacecraft *Mariner 4* took the first close-up pictures of the Martian surface, none of which showed anything that even remotely resembled a canal.

One of the first writers to exploit Lowell's vision was H.G. Wells in *The War of the Worlds* (1898). Wells imagined a race of horrific, octopus-like Martians who were bent on exterminating most of mankind on Earth and enslaving the remainder, so they could move here from their cold, waterless, dying world. The novel was originally published in the United States as a magazine serial, and even before the last installment appeared, a "sequel" was published by American science writer/novelist Garrett P. Serviss. This was *Edison's Conquest of Mars (*1898), in which the great American inventor Thomas Alva Edison in fictional form leads all the world's greatest scientists in a retaliatory attack on the red planet. No one recorded what Edison himself thought of this.

Thus began a kind of "Mars fever." The red planet was all the rage, and countless stories, novels, and articles were published about it. It became everyone's favorite planet.

One author in particular, Edgar Rice Burroughs (1875–1950), was especially inspired by Lowell's Mars and the image of an ancient, dying

---

* Of course they don't exist. Close-up photos of the planet from space probes have shown that there are no canals on Mars. What did Lowell see then? It's been shown that he was probably the victim of a combination of an optical illusion and wishful thinking. There might be some clue in the fact that he also saw canals on just about every other planet he looked at.

After Percival Lowell's *Mars* came out, everyone was creating scenes about Mars, including this 1907 landscape that shows its canals.

planet. Though Burroughs is most probably famous for being the creator of Tarzan, his first book was science fiction, and most of the some seventy books he eventually wrote also fall into that category, including one of the Tarzan stories. After having failed at every position from a gold prospector to a candy salesman, he became a writer as a last resort. His first novel was *A Princess of Mars* (1917; first serialized as *Under the Moons of Mars* in 1912). Unlike Wells's serious *The War of the Worlds,* however, Burroughs's book was filled with nonstop action, adventure, monsters, beautiful princesses, and cliffhanging suspense. It is *science fantasy* in its purest form. Also, unlike Wells, Burroughs never pretended to do anything but entertain. He had no message to impart to his readers other than an invitation for them to have fun. In addition to his long series of novels set on Mars, Burroughs also wrote novels about Pellucidar, a prehistoric world on the inside surface of a hollow Earth, novels set on Venus and on the moon, and novels about many other real and fictional worlds, all of them filled with endless action, bizarre creatures, beautiful princesses, and indestructible heroes. With all of their faults, Burroughs's books are exciting, well-written, and tremendous fun. Perhaps his most lasting contribution to the history of science fiction is the inspiration he provided countless young people, such as Ray Bradbury, who went on to become science fiction authors themselves.

The First Science Fiction Magazines

At the beginning of the twentieth century, almost every magazine published science fiction at one time or another. Of course, these magazines didn't know they were publishing science fiction, and most of the authors didn't know they were writing it. Science fiction as yet didn't even have a name.

Hugo Gernsback (1884–1967) started a magazine, *Modern Electrics,* to help encourage interest in the field and to advertise his products. In order to fill space, he began serializing a story he had written called "Ralph 124C41+"* (1911). Little more than a catalog of the scientific wonders of the year 2660, it proved to be immensely popular. He began publishing similar stories by other authors under the label of "scientific fiction." They became even more popular, and his readers clamored for more. Gernsback, who was not only a wild enthusiast about the future of science and technology but a canny businessman, noticed this increased interest in his own magazine as well as the growing number of scientific stories published in other magazines. It occurred to him that there might be an audience for a publication devoted entirely to this type of fiction. So in April 1926, he founded *Amazing Stories*, the world's first science fiction magazine. He called these types of stories *scientifiction*, a word which apparently no one but Gernsback liked.

Gernsback had very specific ideas about what he thought scientifiction should accomplish. First and foremost, he strongly believed its main purpose was to educate the reader about science and excite him or her about its possibilities. "The formula in all cases," he said, "is that the story must be frankly amazing; second, it must contain a scientific background; third, it must possess originality." Literary quality wasn't even mentioned.

The first issues of *Amazing* contained only reprints of classic stories by Verne, Wells, Poe, and others. Gernsback did this first because he greatly admired these authors and wanted to give his new magazine a serious "literary" feel, and because there just weren't many authors

---

* The title is a pun—if you read it out loud it sounds like "one to foresee for one."

specializing in this writing, especially writers willing to work at the extremely low pay he offered. Many of *Amazing*'s earliest authors came from the ranks of its own readers. What their stories may have lacked in style or quality, they more than made up for in enthusiasm.

The general emphasis—and perhaps even the quality—of the early *Amazing* stories is clearly reflected in the titles of some of the stories: "Monsters of the Ray," "The Machine Man of Ardathia," "The Thought Stealer," "When the Earth Grew Cold," "The Superperfect Bride," "The Comet Doom," "The Moon of Doom," "The Swordsmen of Sardon," and "The Purple Monsters." To Gernsback's credit, he made no distinction between his male and female authors and happily accepted and published stories regardless of the author's gender. The letter column always contained many letters from girls and women who enjoyed the stories.

The quality gradually improved as the writers gained experience, and eventually better writers were attracted to the subject. Among the best was David H. Keller, M.D. (1880–1966), one of the first *Amazing* authors to write stories that weren't exclusively concerned with the mere description of incredible gadgets and scientific wonders. Drawing upon his experience as a psychiatrist, many of Keller's best stories were about how science influenced people's lives and the society they lived in.

Gernsback lost control of *Amazing* in a bankruptcy suit in 1929, but immediately came back with an entirely new rival magazine, *Science Wonder Stories*. In the five years that it lasted, *Wonder Stories* published stories by some of the greatest names in science fiction, including Stanley G. Weinbaum (1902–1935), who contributed revolutionary feats in science fiction.

H.G. Wells had introduced the concept of "aliens" from other

In a scene from J. Schlassel's story "To the Moon by Proxy," a robot is being tested for a space mission by fighting a lion. This first appeared in Gernsback's *Amazing Stories* in October 1928.

worlds, and authors after him depicted these aliens as he did, almost exclusively as hostile, villainous monsters who were single-mindedly devoted to conquest and destruction.* Or if they weren't horrible monsters, they were humans indistinguishable from the people of Earth. Weinbaum changed all of that forever. He introduced the entirely new idea that aliens could not be judged by earthly standards. Aliens would probably not only be physically different from human beings but would also have alien minds, alien intelligences, and alien thoughts along with alien motives. In fact, if they thought so differently, humans might not be able to communicate with them or even understand what they were doing.

In 1930, the first non–Gernsback science fiction magazine appeared: *Astounding Stories*. For the first few years it was not different from *Amazing Stories* or *Wonder Stories*; it published the same sort of super-science adventures. But in 1933, with the advent of a new editor, F. Orlin Tremaine, *Astounding* achieved a dominance in the field. One of Tremaine's innovations was the introduction of "thought variant" stories, which are stories that encourage new and original ideas. Ever since Tremaine, it has maintained its dominance to the present day. (In 1960, it changed its name to *Analog*.) In fact, it is the only science fiction magazine of the 1930s that has been published continuously.

In 1938, twenty-eight-year-old science fiction author John W. Campbell Jr. became editor of *Astounding* and began what many consider to be the "golden age" of science fiction. Campbell worked well with his writers, whom he encouraged and inspired, and maintained

---

* Though other authors had written about aliens from other planets coming to the Earth, these extraterrestrials were almost always human-like and usually friendly. Wells not only made the idea of aliens popular, but he also suggested they might be nonhuman and hostile.

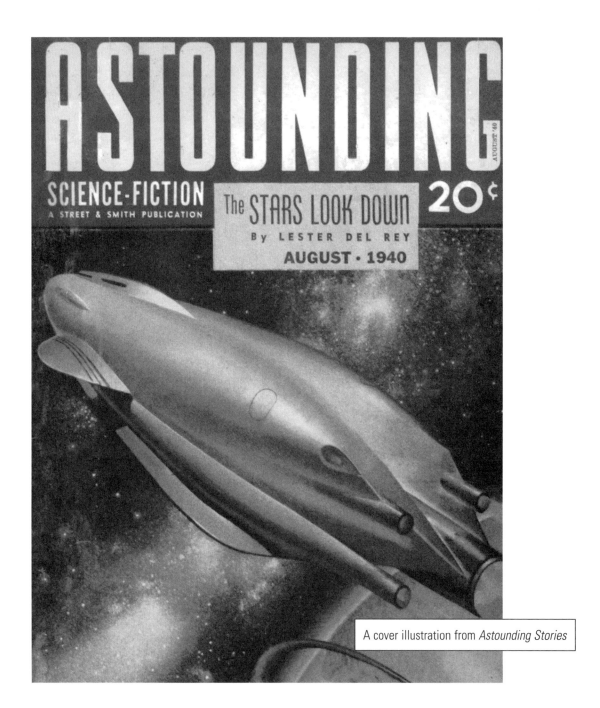

ASTOUNDING
SCIENCE-FICTION
A STREET & SMITH PUBLICATION

AUGUST '40

The STARS LOOK DOWN
By LESTER DEL REY
AUGUST · 1940

20¢

A cover illustration from *Astounding Stories*

Tremaine's "thought variant" policy. He phased out the more old-fashioned themes and absolutely insisted on the highest quality in writing. It was no longer enough that a science fiction story be merely exciting or educational—it also had to be about something. Campbell was so particular and had such high standards that many rival magazines managed to support themselves by accepting the stories he rejected. Most importantly, Campbell turned his attention toward stories that explored the relationship of science and technology with human culture and human psychology. Instead of concentrating on the simple fact of, say, a trip to the moon, an *Astounding* story would ask: what would a society that had space travel be like? How would it be different? What difference would it make to the people making the trip? Author Anthony Boucher summed up Campbell's policy this way: "Grant your gadgets and start your story from there. In other words, assume certain advances in civilization, then work out convincingly just how those would affect the lives of ordinary individuals like you and me . . ." Gone were the superscientists and mad doctors of *Amazing* and its clones, gone were black-and-white struggles between good and evil, gone were the monster alien and evil robot. In their place were ordinary businessmen, engineers, office workers, and the men and women of the spaceship crews.

Perhaps the best example of how science fiction evolved and matured with John Campbell Jr. is the subject of space flight. Originally, a flight into space, to the moon, or to some planet was simply described with little more than a technical account of the science and technology involved. Sometimes an author would use space travel as an excuse to get his or her characters someplace where they could meet evil aliens, beautiful princesses, or horrible monsters.

But space flight in Edmond Hamilton's "What's It Like Out There?," written in 1933, was so different from anything else that the story was almost not published at all. Rejected by nearly every magazine it was sent to, the story didn't find a home until nearly twenty years later in *Astounding*. What made it so shocking to editors was its unrelentingly realistic view that space flight would not be easy and that instead of being filled with adventure and glamour, it might be difficult and dangerous. That difficulty and danger came from bad planning, politics, nature, and even the astronauts themselves. It tells of the first manned expedition to Mars, which is a near disaster because of disease, boredom, mutiny, and technological failures. Hamilton's premise was that the success of space flight wouldn't depend on just having perfect machines: the human factor was equally important, if not more so.

The success of *Astounding* inspired a boom in science fiction magazines and over the next couple of decades there were dozens of titles, most of them lasting only a few issues. All of these magazines were collectively known as "pulps" because of the cheap wood pulp paper on which most of them were printed. The term *pulp fiction* came to mean any lurid, cheap, throwaway story of dubious literary value. This is an unfortunate label. While 90 percent of the writing in the pulps was totally forgettable, the remaining 10 percent represented some of the best, most imaginative writing being published anywhere. Indeed, many great writers, such as the playwright Tennessee Williams, got their start in the pulps.

Science fiction was never the same after John W. Campbell Jr. For one thing, book publishers, who in the past had always shied away from it, began to take it seriously and publish it. Many of Campbell's authors began to see their novels and stories in hard covers. This meant that science fiction was more likely to be seen and read by serious book reviewers; and with good reviews the general public would buy more.

It also meant that it was soon to be found in public libraries where more people could read it. (Most libraries today have a section specially devoted to science fiction.)

An important effect of science fiction publishing was the generation of anthologies, which are book collections of short stories. For the first time, hundreds of excellent stories from the pulps were now available to the general reader. Today there are all kinds of anthologies: collections of stories by a single author, collections based on special themes, stories from one particular magazine or another, best-of-the-year collections, and even anthologies of new, previously unpublished stories.

Weapons and War

In spite of its fascination with the future, science fiction has always reflected the interests and concerns of the time in which it was written. During World War II, science fiction authors looked at the war in science fiction terms, with stories about future wars that paralleled the one then devastating the world and stories about fabulous weapons. There was also a boom in stories of pure escapism that for an afternoon allowed readers to completely forget about a terrible reality. The 1940s saw the birth of the *post-apocalyptic* story. These were usually set in a world that had been ravaged by a cataclysmic war, where civilization had collapsed and the remnants of mankind had reverted to barbarism.

Nuclear or atomic weapons had been a part of science fiction ever since H.G. Wells first coined the word *atomic bomb* in 1914 in his book *The World Set Free.* A cherished story among science fiction fans concerns the time when the FBI invaded John W. Campbell Jr.'s office in 1944, certain that they'd discovered a spy in author Cleve Cartmill. In his short story "Deadline," Cartmill had not only described the effects of an atomic bomb, but got the details of its construction almost exactly right. At that time the Manhattan Project—which was developing America's first atomic bomb—was the most closely guarded secret in history. The agents were sure that someone in the project had leaked information to the author and were ready to arrest Cartmill, Campbell, and anyone else connected with the magazine. Fortunately, Campbell was able to show that his author had used information that had been available to anyone since the 1930s, and that he'd just surmised the rest.

Chapter Four
Science Fiction Today

After the end of World War II, the dominance of the pulp magazines began to end. Already crippled by wartime paper shortages, they faced competition from paperback book publishers. All failed except a very few. Only *Astounding Stories* and *The Magazine of Fantasy and Science Fiction* survive to this day.* This is not to say that the magazines were without influence. They still contributed to the evolution of science fiction.

Earlier science fiction usually concerned itself with how problems could be solved by physical or scientific means. There were few moral

---

* *Astounding Stories* has been published under the name *Analog* since 1960. *Amazing Stories,* the oldest of the science fiction pulps, is still published, but it has not appeared continuously. It has disappeared for months and even years at a time, only to be revived each time by an entirely new publishing company.

or psychological ambiguities: good was usually good, and bad was bad. There was little concern or interest in gray areas. The style that most writers used was equally simple and straightforward. Beginning in the 1950s, science fiction writers made problems more complex; these problems may have social and psychological roots as much as scientific or physical; and that these problems would be best solved by changes in the human psyche or by changes in human society. Many writers, too, were beginning to think that science fiction had become too predictable in subject matter and style and that it was ready for a change. This new trend was much more pessimistic than traditional science fiction and was often antiscience and antitechnology, exhibiting a distrust of both human beings and science. Stories and novels that took on themes like these were termed *new wave*, and they dominated science fiction for many years.

New wave authors emphasized experimentation in style, narration, and subject. J.G. Ballard was one of the earliest contributors. Alfred Bester's *The Demolished Man* (1953) even experimented with the typography of the book itself. Harlan Ellison wrote many hard-core new wave stories, although his primary contribution was as editor of two original new wave anthologies: *Dangerous Visions* (1967) and *Again, Dangerous Visions* (1972). Other authors who experimented were Michael Moorcock, Brian W. Aldiss, and Thomas M. Disch.

Similar to other revolutionary movements, new wave ideas and techniques were eventually absorbed into mainstream science fiction. Perhaps the only place where new wave still shows a highly visible presence is in the relatively new form called *cyberpunk*. Invented almost single-handedly by William Gibson, cyberpunk concerns itself with the relationships between humans and high technology, especially in the computer world of cybernetics. Often very dark, pessimistic, and violent, cyberpunk has been an ideal source for several popular science fiction movies, such as *Blade Runner* (1982) based on a novel by Philip K. Dick, *Johnny Mnemonic* (1995), and *The Maze* (1999). Virtually every movie about the technological world of the near future has been influenced by *Blade Runner*'s dark, richly textured look.

Comic books became a huge outlet for science fiction, especially with the invention of the *graphic novel*—a comic book of longer-than-usual length devoted to telling a single story. Very few of these have been able to stand up with the best of science fiction. Too many depend on the quality of the art rather than the quality of the writing or story ideas. Nevertheless, their popularity has helped turn many readers on to the literature.

Although a few science fiction magazines still existed through the 1960s, only the hardiest ones survived another new idea in publishing: what might be called the *hybrid magazine*. Crossing the science fiction magazine with the science fiction paperback, each book functioned like a magazine. Some of these even came out on a regular basis, just like a magazine. Although the idea of publishing a series of anthologies filled with original, unpublished stories had been tried before in the late 1940s and 1950s, the introduction of the Orbit series of books in 1966 spelled the end for the specialty magazine. The Orbit books, which were usually published quarterly, offered a new market for short story writers—to say nothing of the fact that the publisher usually paid writers much more. The books usually contained stories related by a common theme, such as space travel, telepathy, future war, or ecology.

By the late 1960s, full-time science fiction authors were at last seeing their books appear regularly on best-seller lists. This trend began with two classic books: Frank Herbert's *Dune* (1965) and Robert A. Heinlein's *Stranger in a Strange Land* (1961). From that point on, science fiction entered the awareness of a large part of the

The cover illustration of Frank Herbert's *Dune* by John Schoenherr

reading public, who had previously thought of science fiction as suitable only for children and not to be taken seriously. These new books reached a vast audience of scientists, teachers, students, and mainstream critics who had never before read even a single word of science fiction. Science fiction had finally become respectable and perfectly acceptable to read. It had become "literature."

Science fiction became so respectable that many mainstream authors not only tried their hand at it, but weren't embarrassed at having their books labeled "science fiction." These authors include Ayn Rand *(Anthem, Atlas Shrugged),* Allen Drury *(The Throne of Saturn),* Michael Crichton *(The Andromeda Strain, Jurassic Park, Sphere),* James Michener *(Space),* Anthony Burgess *(A Clockwork Orange),* Kurt Vonnegut *(The Sirens of Titan, Slaughterhouse-Five),* and Carl Sagan *(Contact).*

Science fiction has become enormously popular, accounting for more than 20 percent of all fiction now being published. Science fiction has also become big business.

The Great Writers

The great editors may have been instrumental in shaping the direction of science fiction, but the men and women who wrote it gave it form and substance. During the first century of science fiction publishing in the United States, a number of notable writers were particularly instrumental in helping to define modern science fiction.

If Edgar Rice Burroughs introduced interplanetary settings to science fiction, E.E. Smith, Ph.D. (1890–1965) expanded its scope to the entire galaxy, and even beyond. Inventing *space opera* virtually single-handedly, Smith's series of interconnected novels, in which mile-long spaceships battled against entire planets, ranged across thousands of years of time and millions of light-years of space. His best-known series are the Lensmen books—*Triplanetary* (1934–35/1948), *First Lensman* (1950), *Galactic Patrol* (1937/1950), *Gray Lensman* (1939/1951), *Second Stage Lensman* (1941–42/1953) and *Children of the Lens* (1947–48/1954). The books describe an epic struggle, lasting millions of years, between two ancient galactic races who use newer species, such as human beings, to their own ends. No other author has ever approached the grand scale of Smith's epic saga.

Before he began his career as editor of *Astounding Stories*, John W. Campbell Jr. (1910–1971) wrote science fiction. Though much of it was in the superscience planet-busting vein of E.E. Smith, he eventually produced some highly original, influential stories in his own right. His story "Twilight" (1934) was narrated by a man at a time when Earth was at its end, when the sun itself was dying and human beings had been long extinct. While echoing part of H.G. Wells's *The Time Machine,* "Twilight" was entirely different from anything that had been published in the Gernsback–dominated pulps. Perhaps his most famous story is "Who Goes There?" (1938). The basis for the classic film *The Thing* (1951, remade in 1982), "Who Goes There?" tells about a small group of men at an Antarctic base who are stalked by a shape-changing alien who may have taken the form of any one of them.

Robert A. Heinlein (1907–1988) began his science fiction career in the pages of Campbell's *Astounding* and continued producing stories and best-selling novels clear up to his death in 1988. His literary longevity might lie in the fact that he was never content to rely on a single style. It seemed as though whenever he achieved success with one type of story or novel, he would suddenly veer off into a wholly unexpected direction and write something completely different for his next book. Some of his very best science fiction is contained in a series of juvenile novels he wrote between 1947 and 1959. An aspect of science fiction that Heinlein pioneered (though the idea goes back further than E.E. Smith) is the "future history." This is where an author bases all of his or her stories and novels on a preconceived background, as though they reflect a "real" history that has not yet occurred.

Frank Herbert (1920–1986) made a major contribution to science fiction with a series of books that began with his classic novel *Dune* (1965). One of the best-selling science fiction novels of all time, *Dune* has developed a fiercely loyal cult following. It was one of the first science fiction novels to become widely popular among mainstream readers, people who ordinarily might not have read a science fiction novel. In doing so it was instrumental in making science fiction "acceptable."

Isaac Asimov (1920–1992) was yet another graduate of *Astounding*. His contribution to science fiction lies in two major creations. The first, inspired by the story of the rise and fall of the Roman Empire, is the sprawling Foundation Trilogy (1951–1953), which tells the story of the fall of a galactic empire and the efforts made by one man to shorten the millennia of barbarianism he knows he must follow. His second contribution has been even more significant. First delineated in a series of stories collected in the book *I, Robot* (1950), the "Laws of Robotics" have been used by scores of writers ever since. These laws are: 1. A robot may not injure a human being, or, through inaction, allow a human being to come to harm; 2. A robot must obey the orders given it by human beings except where such orders would conflict with the First Law; 3. A robot must protect its own existence as long as such protection does not conflict with the First or Second Law. The film *Bicentennial Man* (1999) was based on one of Asimov's robot stories.

Arthur C. Clarke (b. 1917) is a British writer with one of the longest

Sir Arthur C. Clarke

and most successful science fiction careers. Perhaps best known for the film *2001: A Space Odyssey,* which he cocreated with director Stanley Kubrick, Clarke is a *hard science* writer whose books have a strong grounding in real science. One of his most common themes is the spiritual enlightenment of humankind in the face of technological or natural adversity. In one of Clarke's own favorite stories, "Transit of Earth" (1972), the first astronaut on Mars is dying. As he records his impressions of watching the Earth move across the face of the sun, he realizes that in spite of his personal tragedy it is still a great moment for human beings.

Ray Bradbury (b. 1920) is almost an antiscience fiction writer. Few of his stories are based on any sort of science or technology, and when they are, science is seldom treated sympathetically. Many of his stories are a nostalgic longing for a simpler time in the past, when machines were not as intrusive as they are now. Bradbury's books are known for their beautiful, poetic writing, and of all science fiction writers mainstream readers have accepted him the most. He was one of the first science fiction writers to be published in non–science fiction magazines. Two of his most famous books are *The Martian Chronicles* (1950) and *Fahrenheit 451* (1953). The first is a collection of short stories about the first human colonists on Mars. The second book is about a chilling time in the near future when books are outlawed, and "firemen" go from house to house searching for books and then burning them. The title refers to the temperature at which book paper begins to burn.

The fame of Hal Clement (pseudonym of Harry Stubbs) (b. 1922) rests on a relatively small number of novels, most notably *Needle* (1950), *Iceworld* (1953), and *Mission of Gravity* (1954). Clement's books are filled with realistic depictions of extraordinary aliens described with the eye of a scientist. Even though his aliens and their worlds are as scientifically accurate as he can possibly make them, Clement's stories are never bogged down by cold fact. His ideas are always original and thought-provoking. *Needle,* for example, is a detective story in which the protagonist, a kind of alien policeman, is searching for an escaped alien criminal. The only problem is that both aliens can only live inside host bodies—in this case two human beings. The problem: how to find *which* human among the billions on Earth is harboring the criminal. In *Iceworld* we see our own planet as an alien world. It's told almost entirely through the eyes of an alien explorer from a world so hot that he breathes gaseous sulfur. He cannot imagine life existing on a planet so cold that tin and lead are frozen solid.

Women in Science Fiction

For many years science fiction was thought to be written by men for male readers. In the stories of the 1920s, 30s, 40s, and 50s, the stereotypical image of science fiction was that of a space-suited male hero fighting off a fearsome bug-eyed monster while holding a swooning girl in one arm. When female characters did appear, they usually existed only to be rescued. If a strong female appeared in a story, she was invariably depicted as an evil villain who was eventually overcome by the hero. The truth is that women writers and readers have been part of science fiction even before science fiction had a name.

In many ways, science fiction's sexist reputation has been unfair. Historically, it has been no more sexist than any other literary genre—such as detective stories, romances, or Westerns—and far less than most. There have always been female authors as well as very strong female characters.

One of the most popular female writers in the early pulp days of science fiction was Catherine L. Moore (1911–1987). She wrote a long series of science fiction stories during the 1930s and 40s about a futuristic adventurer named Northwest Smith, and fantasies about a female warrior named Jirel of Joiry. Leigh Brackett (1915–1978) specialized in space opera and much later went on to write the screenplay for *The Empire Strikes Back.* Marion Zimmer Bradley (1930–1999) also wrote high adventure stories, but later in her career wrote stories that explored women's interests, especially in her very popular Darkover series. Perhaps one of the most popular, best-selling science fiction authors of all time is Andre Norton (b. 1912). Since the early 1950s, she continues to publish novels.

Some have speculated that many early women writers had been accepted by men readers because of the ambiguity of their names. It was hard to tell whether C.L. Moore, Leigh Brackett, or Andre Norton were male or female. This may or may not have been true. But it is true that when science fiction authors with clearly female names—such as Katherine MacLean or Judith Merril—began publishing their work, they were accepted by fans just as eagerly as male authors.

The end of the 1950s saw increasing numbers of women writers entering the field. Many of them were attracted to the increasing interest in the social sciences and psychology. By the end of the following decade, these women became a major presence. Judith Merril, in her role as the editor of a series of anthologies, was instrumental in popularizing the *new wave* style of writing. Coincidentally, the rise in the number of women science fiction writers during the 1960s occurred during the rise in feminism and women's rights. A great many women writers used the unique quality of science fiction to explore social issues. Many stories and novels were very politically feminist in slant, while others were content to simply show strong female characters in important, sympathetic roles.

Women writers are as good and as popular as any of their male counterparts. Among the best are Anne McCaffrey (b. 1926), a

Fifteen stories by the world's Great
Writers of Science-Fantasy . . . for the
first time in any Anthology

A LION ORIGINAL

25c

HUMAN?

edited by
JUDITH MERRIL

With
an introduction
by
FREDRIC BROWN
205

The cover of *Human?*,
a new wave
anthology, edited
by Judith Merril

writer of traditional science fiction who may be best known for her series of novels about the dragonriders of Pern. Like Frank Herbert and the planet Arrakis of *Dune*, McCaffrey made Pern a very real world with a fully realized history, politics, and social structure. Human beings on Pern develop a kind of telepathic relationship with the native dragons that is necessary for the survival of both species. McCaffrey won a Hugo Award, the equivalent of the Academy Award for science fiction, for her work. She was the first woman to win it. In her famous short story, "The Ship Who Sang," McCaffrey tells the poignant story of a girl, Helva, who suffers from such debilitating birth defects that her brain is removed from her body and placed into the circuitry of a spaceship. Helva becomes the ship's "brain" and the ship becomes her "body." The story revolves around her relationship with—and love of—the sole human being on board.

Joan D. Vinge (b. 1948) is best known for her novel *The Snow Queen* (1980) and its sequels. A trained anthropologist, Vinge describes her fiction as being "anthropological science fiction, with an emphasis on the interaction of different cultures (human and alien), and of individual people to their horizons." She has also written a science fiction novel, *Psion* (1982), for young people.

Ursula K. Le Guin (b. 1929), a writer of both science fiction and fantasy, is the daughter of an anthropologist and a writer of children's books. Among her most popular novels are *The Lathe of Heaven* (1971), in which a man's dreams determine what the world becomes like, and the Earthsea series (1968-1990) for young people. All of her stories show a great concern for human and social issues.

Today, there is no real way to categorize "female" science fiction. Women writers are producing books in every area, from hard science stories to outright fantasy.

ANDRE NORTON

THE LAST PLANET

ORIGINAL TITLE: STAR RANGERS

"ONE OF THE BEST SCIENCE-FICTION NOVELS TO APPEAR THIS SEASON."
—Springfield Republican

ACE BOOK
D-542
35c

The cover of Andre Norton's *The Last Planet*

A scene from
James Gurney's
Dinotopia

Science Fiction for Young People

With the almost universal popularity of science fiction among young readers and its increasing acceptance by parents and teachers, there have been increasing numbers of science fiction books written specially for children; many of them are so good that adults enjoy them, too. Robert Heinlein's juvenile science fiction books started this trend. Also, many "adult" science fiction books—especially those by E.E. Smith, Isaac Asimov, and Arthur C. Clarke—can be read with just as much enjoyment by younger readers.

Andre Norton has written scores of books for younger readers. Many of her science fiction books often combine magic with scientific explanations as well as paranormal abilities. In 1983 she became the first woman author to be honored with a Grand Master Nebula Award, given by the Science Fiction Writer's Association for her lifetime achievement. Ursula K. Le Guin's Earthsea series, which began with *The Wizard of Earthsea* (1968), is often regarded as an outstanding collection of books for young readers that combines elements of fantasy and science fiction.

Diana Wynne Jones has written a number of excellent science fiction novels for young readers, including *The Homeward Bounders* (1981) and *A Tale of Time City* (1987). These deal with some of the strange paradoxes involved in time travel. Robert C. O'Brien's *Mrs. Frisby and the Rats of NIMH* (1971) is about laboratory rats who have had their intelligence artificially boosted, and O'Brien's *Z for Zachariah* (1975) is a moving and often scary novel about a world devastated by nuclear war. Terry Pratchett has written a series of very funny novels, beginning with *Truckers* (1989) about aliens trying to live among human beings. Artist-author James Gurney has published two lavishly illustrated books set in his imaginary world of Dinotopia—*Dinotopia* (1992) and *The World Beneath* (1997)— where human beings and intelligent dinosaurs live together peacefully. In addition to these books, other authors have written stories set in the Dinotopia "universe."

Some of the best science fiction novels for young people are those by Laurence Yep, Robert O'Brien, Cherry Wilder, John Christopher, and Madeleine L'Engle, whose wonderful *A Wrinkle in Time* (1962) has been cherished by many children.

Science Fiction Tomorrow

Can one predict the future of the literature of the future? Probably not— at least not with any more success than predicting anything else. But there are some ongoing trends that are worth thinking about. Perhaps the biggest change in science fiction between 1950 and the present day is its move from cult interest to big business. It has never had as large an audience, nor as much critical and popular acceptance, as it has now. In some ways this might not be good for science fiction, as the lines between it and mainstream literature become ever more blurred. As science fiction author and historian James Gunn suggests, what were once distinct categories of literature are becoming more like the colors in the spectrum, one merging imperceptibly into another. As it becomes more and more difficult to separate "true" science fiction from other types of literature, will science fiction be able to maintain its individuality? Another problem is that the ratio of bad science fiction to good science fiction gets higher and higher; the chance of picking a book at random and having it be a bad one is increasing. But at the same time that bad science fiction keeps getting worse, good science fiction keeps getting better, even if it is sometimes harder to find in the flood of terrible books.

Science fiction's popularity may work against it, too. As more and more writers work in the field for more and more of the same publishers, science fiction may begin to suffer from the lack of strong influences. An individual editor, such as John W. Campbell Jr., or a single author can no longer influence its shape and direction.

Nevertheless, all of the old subcategories of science fiction seem to be going as strong as ever: authors are still writing everything from science fantasy to space opera to hard science fiction to science adventure, and readers eagerly buy and read their books and stories. The books of classic authors are being reprinted and are no less popular with new readers than they were with old ones. Younger and younger readers are starting to read science fiction, too, and many writers have made a specialty of creating science fiction for them.

All in all, the future of science fiction has never looked more exciting.

Chapter Five
The Great Themes and Ideas

Almost all of the main themes in science fiction were created in the 1920s and 1930s. During the years since, while science fiction has explored every avenue and corner of science and technology, and has told its stories in scores of different styles, some special themes have stood out and have made science fiction unique.

Galactic Empires

In the late 1920s, Jack Williamson, the author of *The Legion of Space* novels, introduced a theme that the billions of stars and planets of the Milky Way galaxy might be united in a single federation. This theme, called the galactic empire, was little more than an ill-defined backdrop for a story's plot, similar to how Western movies used the Old West; you never learned much about it. However, when Isaac Asimov created his Foundation Trilogy—*Foundation* (1951), *Foundation and Empire*

the foundation trilogy

by Isaac Asimov

Three Classics of Science Fiction

FOUNDATION

FOUNDATION and EMPIRE

SECOND FOUNDATION

The cover of Isaac Asimov's *The Foundation Trilogy*

(1952), and *Second Foundation* (1953)—he reinvented the galactic empire. Using the history of the Roman Empire as his model, Asimov not only made a galactic empire the background for the entire series, but he also used it as a historic cornerstone for the story's world, around which everyone and everything revolved.

In his series Asimov proposed the science of *psychohistory*, a branch of mathematics and statistics that has the ability to predict the future. Two rival "foundations" are created by the founder of psychohistory to rebuild civilization after its collapse, which psychohistory has foretold. Without the help of the foundations, it would take thirty thousand years to recreate civilization, but only one thousand years with them. As the scientist explains:

> *"The Empire . . . has stood twelve thousand years. The dark ages to come will endure not twelve but thirty thousand years. A Second Empire will rise, but between it and our civilization will be one thousand generations of suffering humanity. We must fight that . . . I do not say that we can prevent the fall. But it is not yet too late to shorten the interregnum that will follow. It is possible, gentlemen, to reduce the duration of anarchy to a single millennium, if my group is allowed to act now. We are at a delicate moment in history. The huge, onrushing mass of events must be deflected just a little—just a little— It cannot be much, but it may be enough to remove twenty-nine thousand years of misery from human history."*

Since then, many writers who have written stories involving galactic empires have tried to make them realistic, imagining just how such a huge government might actually work and what its problems might be. Most modern science fiction authors have come to realize that the sheer distances involved—to say nothing of the number of planets—in a truly galaxy-wide empire would make it very unstable. It would probably collapse for the same reasons the Roman Empire did: it would be too big to administer. Stories about galactic empires are scarce. Most writers confine themselves to smaller portions of a galaxy, such as the Federation of Planets in *Star Trek.*

Space Opera

Although space opera is one of the most old-fashioned themes of science fiction, it remains very popular. The *Star Wars* series, for example, is pure space opera out of the golden age of science fiction of the 1930s and 1940s. Space opera is closely related to the theme of galactic empires, since it requires such vast backdrops. Usually mythic in proportions, they deal with issues of good versus evil in very fundamental terms. Its heroes and heroines fight superhuman battles against overwhelming odds. Unlike the ancient Greek myths, which space opera most resembles, these heroes often use their knowledge of science and engineering, and sometimes their superior physical strength, to defeat their enemies without any supernatural or magical powers (though they are very often psychic).

Edmond Hamilton (1904-1977) penned some of the first true space operas. In his stories of the Interstellar Patrol, his heroes defend their federation of planets against alien invaders and interstellar treachery. E.E. Smith, however, perfected this form in his famous Lensmen series. Written as a continuous story, these novels describe a vast battle between good and evil that not only span our entire galaxy but thousands of years of time. Although written between forty and fifty years ago, the Lensmen series has been enormously popular and is still being read today.

Perhaps the best way to give some idea of the character of true space opera is to quote from a part of Smith's *Gray Lensman* (1951), in which the villains' planet is destroyed by smashing it between two other planets:

"The two worlds rushed together, doomed Jarnevon squarely between them. Haynes snapped out his order as the three were within two seconds of contact; and as he spoke all the pressors and all the tractors were released. The ships of the Patrol were already free— none had been inert since leaving Jalte's explanet—and thus could not be harmed by flying debris.

The planets touched. They coalesced, squishingly at first, the encircling warships drifting lightly away before a cosmically violent blast of superheated atmosphere. Jarnevon burst open, all the way around, and spattered; billions upon billions of tons of hot core-magma being hurled afar in gouts and streamers. The two planets, crashing through what had been a world, met, crunched, crushed together in all the unimaginable momentum of their masses and velocities. They subsided, crashingly. Not merely mountains, but entire halves of worlds disrupted and fell, in such Gargantuan paroxysms as the eye of man had never elsewhere beheld. And every motion generated heat. The kinetic energy of translation of two worlds became heat. Heat added to heat, piling up ragingly, frantically, unable to escape!

The masses, still falling upon and through and past themselves and each other melted—boiled—vaporized incandescently. The entire mass, the mass of three fused worlds, began to equilibrate; growing hotter and hotter as more and more of its terrific motion was converted into pure heat. Hotter! Hotter! HOTTER!"

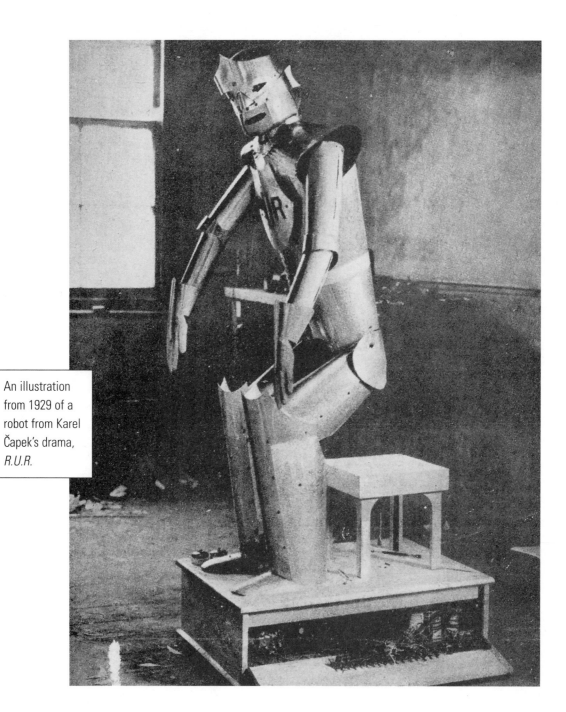

An illustration from 1929 of a robot from Karel Čapek's drama, *R.U.R.*

Robots, Computers, and Cyborgs

Robot entered the language through a science fiction play by the Czech playwright, Karel Čapek: *R.U.R.* (1921). "R.U.R." stood for "Rossum's Universal Robots," and "robot" came from the Czech word for "slave." In the play, Čapek's robots are really artificial human beings, what today would be called *androids*. In modern use, robot is usually reserved for a wholly artificial device that imitates human behavior.

Robots had appeared in fiction before Čapek's play, of course. E.T.A. Hoffman wrote about a beautiful dancing automaton in "The Sandman" (1817); Nathanial Hawthorne featured a mechanical butterfly in "The Artist of the Beautiful" (1844); mechanical men appeared in Fitz-James O'Brien's "Wondersmith" (1859); and the first robot that turned on its creator appeared in "Moxon's Master" by Ambrose Bierce (1909).

Long before robots existed in reality, science fiction writers appreciated some of their potential dangers. David H. Keller wrote several stories in the 1920s in which he warned of the hazards of relying too much on robot assistance, warning of the possibility that they might eventually take over even the most human of occupations. This was a fear that was expressed in dozens of science fiction stories: robots might someday come to replace human beings altogether. There were even stories about robot societies existing long after mankind had become extinct, making them wonder whether human beings ever really existed or if they were simply a childish myth.

Isaac Asimov developed his idea of the three "Laws of Robotics" in his series of robot stories and novels. The limitations these laws placed on the behavior and actions of robots—which until then were almost always treated as nothing more than mechanical people—opened up whole new story possibilities for many authors, who were quick to adopt Asimov's "laws." Asimov continued exploring many of the themes from his earlier books, such as *I, Robot* (1950), *The Naked Sun* (1956), and in more recent novels, *The Robots of Dawn* (1983) and *Robots and Empire* (1985).

Some writers made robots threatening by working within Asimov's laws. For example, in Jack Williamson's "With Folded Hands" (1947; later as the novel *The Humanoids,* 1949), robots are so obsessed with protecting humans from any possible harm that they literally kill them with kindness.

Androids (from a Greek word meaning "manlike") are artificial human beings. Since androids resemble human beings very closely, it's possible that they would desire the same human status and privileges. Data from the television series *Star Trek: The Next Generation* is probably the best-known android. Philip K. Dick probably wrote more stories about androids than anyone else. His novel *Do Androids Dream of Electric Sheep?* (1968), which was adapted as the motion picture *Blade Runner*, is about a group of androids who desperately want to be accepted as human beings. Stories such as these deeply concern themselves with what it actually means to be human. In an essay written in 1973, Dick wrote, "Someday a human being may shoot a robot which has come out of a General Electric factory and, to his surprise, see it weep and bleed. And the dying robot may shoot back and, to its surprise, see a wisp of gray smoke arise from the electric pump that it supposed was the human's beating heart. It would be a great moment of truth for both of them."

Cyborgs are human-machine hybrids—part machine, part human. The idea of cyborgs, short for "cybernetic organism," is fairly new to science fiction. In *Who?,* by Algis Budrys (1958), a scientist is partially rebuilt as a machine after an explosion, and he has to prove that he is who he says he is. Frederik Pohl's *Man Plus* (1976) describes a man

In *Star Trek: The Next Generation* episode "Best of Both Worlds," Captain Picard (Patrick Stewart) is assimilated into the Borg and becomes Locutus, leader of the cyborg civilization.

who is almost completely rebuilt as a machine in order to survive unprotected on Mars. C.L. Moore's "No Woman Born" (1944) is about a famed dancer who is so badly crippled she can no longer perform. When her brain is transplanted into the body of a robot, she not only is able to make a comeback but becomes a better dancer. Later, she wonders whether her link with humanity is lost when she realizes that the man who built her may not be able to build another of her kind. In the television series *Star Trek: The Next Generation* and *Star Trek: Voyager*, the Borgs, short for cyborg, are probably the best-known cyborgs today.

Robots have enabled science fiction to explore what it means to be "human." Is it the shape and nature of one's body that determines whether you are human or not? Or is the mind—or perhaps even the "soul"—the most important thing? The idea that a person's body is the least important thing about a person is the theme of stories like "No Woman Born" and "The Ship Who Sang." But in both of those stories the "mind" of the machine is still a human brain. Could this be taken a step further? Could a "human" mind exist in a machine brain? Eando Binder's "I, Robot" (1939) was one of the first stories to wonder if there might someday be such a blurring in the distinction between human and machine, and perhaps that such distinctions may not even be possible in the future. The story is the autobiography of Adam Link, a robot, told in his own words. When he is hunted down by a mob convinced that he is guilty of the murder of his creator, Link kills himself. "Ironic, isn't it," he asks at the end, "that I have the very feelings you are so sure I lack?"

Time Travel and Alternate History

Before H.G. Wells a few authors had touched on the theme of traveling in time. Mark Twain's hero in *A Connecticut Yankee in King Arthur's*

Court (1889) is sent back to feudal England by a lightning bolt, and Ebeneezer Scrooge in Charles Dickens's *A Christmas Carol* (1843) is taken to his past, present, and future by a trio of ghosts. But in his book *The Time Machine* (1895), Wells provided a science fictional explanation of how time travel might work. He used a machine instead of using the supernatural.

Since then, hundreds of writers have had a great deal of fun exploring the theme of time travel, especially creating the strange paradoxes that could arise. For example, what would happen if you were to go into the past and prevent your parents from ever meeting? If they didn't meet, they couldn't have any children; if they didn't have children, you were never born . . . but if you weren't born there couldn't be anyone to go into the past to keep your parents from getting married! In one famous story, "All You Zombies," Robert Heinlein's hero solves the problem by becoming his own mother and father. In another of the most puzzling time paradox stories, "As Never Was" by P. Schyler Miller, a time traveler returns from the distant future with a strange, beautiful knife. Unfortunately, he dies before he can tell anyone where it came from, so the knife is put into a museum. For years other time travelers search the future, trying to find the source of the knife until finally one person succeeds. Thousands of years from now that person finds the footprints of the original time traveler leading to the ruins of a great building. They lead to a shattered glass case and in the dust is the outline of the knife. Now the answer is clear: the first time traveler had gone into the future and gotten the knife from the ruins of the museum into which it had been put in the past. The question is, however, where did the knife come from in the first place?

Some stories employ the theme of *time dilation*. What happens when you travel near the speed of light? Would a space traveler return to the Earth younger than his or her twin who remained home? If the space-

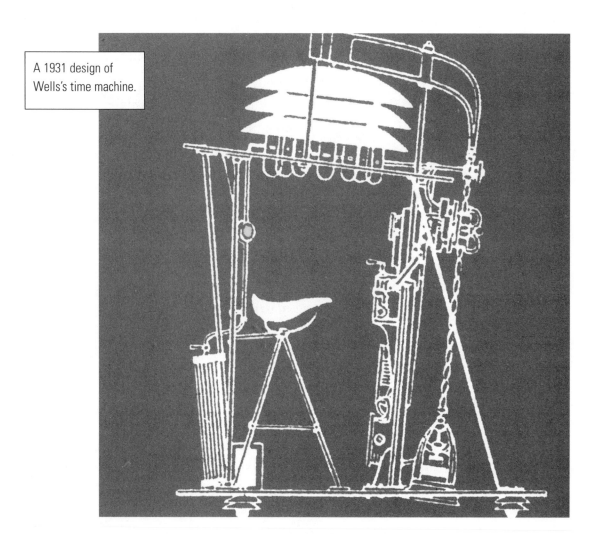

traveling twin stayed away long enough and went fast enough, the difference in age might be days, months, years, or possibly even centuries. A good example of a time dilation story, and one involving twin brothers, is Robert A. Heinlein's *Time for the Stars* (1956).

Recent books that have treated time traveling both seriously and with a sense of fun include Simon Hawkes's Timewar series, beginning with *The Ivanhoe Gambit* (1984), and Julian May's series that begins with *The Many-Colored Land* (1981). Of all the classic themes of science fiction, time travel is one of the very few that has shown no sign of aging or diminishing in popularity.

A distant relative of the time travel theme is that of *alternate history*. Stories using this theme ask what would happen if a certain event in history had happened differently. Ward Moore's *Bring the Jubilee* (1953) wonders what today's world would be like if the South had won the Civil War. Philip K. Dick's *The Man in the High Castle* (1962) takes place in a United States that has lost World War II and is now occupied by Germany and Japan.

Another variation is the *alternate world* theme. It differs slightly from alternate history in that it speculates on the possibility of "parallel worlds." At every turning point in history, an entirely new and different universe is created so that every possibility takes place. Instead of just one word in which Columbus discovered America, there are two worlds: one in which he discovered America and the other in which he did not.

Recently, author Harry Turtledove has specialized in alternate histories and has written a long series of popular novels, such as *A Different Flesh* (1988) and *A World of Difference* (1989), that ask "what if" some event in history had happened differently. Imagine the changes that might take place in our present if even a very small change were to be made in the past; it's a good way to understand how history works.

Space Travel and Exploration

Space travel is one of the oldest themes in science fiction. In fact, space travel is so closely identified with science fiction that many people think that it's the *only* subject in science fiction. When *Apollo 11* made

An illustration by A. de Neuville from the first French edition of Verne's *From the Earth to the Moon*. The space projectile fires its retro rockets. Verne was the first to suggest the use of rockets in spaceflight.

the first landing on the moon in 1969, the question science fiction authors were asked most was: "What are you going to write about now?"

During the first half of the twentieth century, most space travel fiction limited itself to the worlds of our solar system and about the journey of travelling itself. The Earth's moon was the most popular destination for years, followed closely by Mars, no doubt because of the influence of Percival Lowell's books. Some authors described the exploration of these worlds with great attention to accuracy, while others, such as Edgar Rice Burroughs, could care less about reality and used the planets merely as exotic backgrounds for tales of high adventure.

But once it became clear that space travel could really happen, writers wrote more about the consequences of space exploration: how long journeys in a spaceship would affect a small crew, or how colonists would survive on an alien planet. Space travel soon went beyond the planets of our solar system as authors devised imaginary methods for traveling to the stars.

Then, after Einstein proved that it would be impossible to travel faster than the speed of light (which would make a one-way journey just to the nearest star more than four years long),* writers have been extremely clever in suggesting ways to get around this restriction. They invented all sorts of hyperdrives, matter transmitters, and space warps.

Several authors explored the idea of a "generation starship," an enormous ship capable of carrying hundreds, perhaps even thousands, of people. Traveling very fast would not be necessary since the passengers

---

*The nearest star to Earth is Proxima Centauri, which would take a spaceship traveling at the speed of light—186,000 miles per second—4.3 years to reach.

leaving Earth would never live to see it arrive at its destination. If necessary, the journey could take centuries, and only the distant descendants of the original astronauts would see the end of the trip. What might it be like to live an entire life—from birth to death—on board a huge spaceship? What if the descendants of the original passengers decided they didn't want to colonize another world? In Robert Heinlein's "Universe" (1941), the people inside an enormous generation ship have forgotten the original mission and don't even realize that they are on board a spaceship. The person who makes the incredible discovery that this "universe" is only a spaceship and that a much greater universe lies outside is labeled a heretic and is nearly condemned to death.

By the end of the twentieth century, few science fiction novels were about space travel. As a subject it became as commonplace as horses and wagon trains were in Western novels. Also, writers didn't concern themselves too much with stories about the future of space exploration. Novels and stories about the first landings on the moon or on faraway planets seemed old-fashioned. However, recent NASA space probes to Mars and other planets in the solar system began to revive interest in our immediate backyard, and serious proposals for manned missions to Mars re-excited interest in realistic stories about space travel set in the near future. Because of this excitement, many novels appeared: *Menace Under Marswood* (1983) by Sterling Lanier; *Frontera* (1984) by Lewis Shiner; *Mars* (1992) by Ben Bova; *Labyrinth of Night* (1992) by Allan Steele; and—one of the great works of science fiction to come out of the 1990s—the Mars trilogy by Kim Stanley Robinson. Robinson's *Red Mars* (1992) *Green Mars* (1993), and *Blue Mars* (1994) cover the history of the exploration and colonization of Mars from the first manned landing to the not-so-distant future when Mars is in the process of being terraformed into an Earth-like world.

Writers eventually started setting stories on worlds around other suns than our own. The possibility of planets orbiting binary stars, red giants, neutron stars, and other exotic objects allowed writers to imagine worlds far stranger than those in their own solar system. In "Nightfall" (1941), Isaac Asimov wondered what it might be like to live on a world near the center of a star cluster: a world that would never know the meaning of "night" since there would always be at least one sun in its sky. Asimov imagined what would happen if in every few thousand years everything lined up just right so that night *did* fall on the planet, its people saw a black sky filled with stars, and realized for the first time how vast the universe was.

The master of inventing new worlds may be Hal Clement. The most famous of these is the planet Mesklin in *Mission of Gravity* (1954). The gravity at the equator on this world is seven hundred times that of the Earth—an environment that is far too strong for a human to live and work in. (Mesklin is a very strange world indeed. It rotates very rapidly—its day is only eighteen minutes long—so the planet is flattened to the shape of a hamburger bun. This flattening means that its gravity is not the same all over. While the gravity is seven hundred times that of the Earth at the equator, where Mesklin is thickest, it is only three times as great at the poles.) So how do we recover a space probe lost on the planet? We recruit the help of the local inhabitants: fifteen-inch intelligent centipedes.

Another way of inventing new worlds that has even become something of a popular semiserious "game" is called "world building." Several writers, scientists, and artists will gather together to create a new world from scratch. After setting certain conditions, such as the type of star the world belongs to, they will try to make their new planet as realistic as possible. An enormous, and sometimes surprising, number of factors have to be taken into consideration, especially if one wants life to evolve on the planet. For example, if this world orbits near a very hot star, it would be unlikely to have a climate like the Earth's. Sometimes these newly created imaginary worlds become so interesting that stories and novels end up being written around them.

Future War

Science fiction has had a fascination with warfare for more than a century. The first significant example of a fictional future war *The Battle of Dorking* (1871) by Colonel George Chesney. The description of a German invasion into England is so realistic that at the time it actually inspired renovations in Britain's military. Most future war novels followed Chesney's pattern and usually described an invasion of the author's homeland by whatever country was currently in disfavor. Sometimes it wasn't merely another nation but an entire race, and many future war novels became extremely racist. For example, a century ago many novels warned of a possible attack from China or Japan, which is how the phrase "yellow peril" entered into the language.

Other authors have been less concerned with whom future wars might be fought, and more concerned with what such wars might be like and what they would mean to ordinary people. Robert A. Heinlein's *Starship Troopers* (1959) described a world in which a war with an alien race had virtually taken over society. People who had not served in the military were not considered citizens and couldn't vote. When asked what the difference was between a soldier and a civilian, a student replied: "The difference . . . lies in the field of civic virtue. A soldier accepts personal responsibility for the safety of the body politic of which he is a member, defending it. The civilian does not."

The hero and heroine of Joe Haldeman's *The Forever War* (1974) have to deal with not only an interstellar war but the problems of time dilation. In traveling from star to star at near light speeds, the hero ages only months while years and centuries pass on Earth. Worse, because the war is being fought at many different places in the galaxy, time is passing at different rates for everyone—weeks here, months there, years elsewhere. In order to "catch up" in time with her lover, Bill, the heroine, Marygay Potter, has to go to special lengths, as she explains in a letter to him:

> ". . . I know from the records that you're out at Sade-138 and won't be back for a couple of centuries. No problem . . . It took all my money, and all the money of five other old-timers, but we bought a cruiser from UNEF. And we're using it as a time machine.
>
> So I'm on a relativistic shuttle, waiting for you. All it does is go out five light years and come back to Middle Finger, very fast. Every ten years I age about a month. So if you're on schedule and still alive, I'll only be twenty-eight when you get here. Hurry!
>
> I never found anybody else and I don't want anybody else. I don't care whether you're ninety years old or thirty. If I can't be your lover, I'll be your nurse."

Other novels that demonstrate a trend toward very militaristic books about future war are a series of books by David A. Drake that begins with *Hammer's Slammers* (1979) and the Man-Kzin Wars series (1988–1991) by Larry Niven.

Supermen

The evolution of the human being, physically and mentally, is one of the most important themes in science fiction. Authors have had to con-

An illustration by
Stephen Hickman
for Larry Niven's
Man-Kzin Wars
series

sider: what powers would constitute true superiority? What advantages would they have? What disadvantages? How would someone cope with them? How would society cope with a superior being? What sort of world would a society of superhumans create?

Human beings endowed with extraordinary powers—physical or mental—are hardly new to fiction. Examples can be found as far back as ancient mythology, such as Hercules. But not until the theories of Charles Darwin had authors begun to think about the evolution of human beings. Some early attempts were H.G. Wells's *The Food of the Gods* (1904) and J.D. Beresford's *The Hampdenshire Wonder* (1911). Philip Wylie, in *Gladiator* (1931), told the story of a man of normal intelligence possessed with superhuman strength. It was the inspiration for the creators of *Superman*. But the first attempt to realistically describe what it might be like to have a superhuman intelligence was *Odd John* (1935) by Olaf Stapledon. Later stories, especially those written during the late 1940s and 1950s, dealt not so much with superintelligence or superstrength, but with unusual mental powers, such as ESP.

Most stories about superhumans deal with the problems they have while existing in a world of "normal" people. Very often he or she is ostracized, or even hunted down and killed. Sometimes the superman becomes the villain, seeing his fellow citizens as mere subhumans, as in Frank Robinson's *The Power* (1956). An unusual twist in some stories is that some "super" ability is normal and everyone has it. In Alfred Bester's *The Demolished Man* (1953), everyone has the ability to read minds. The hero has to discover a way to commit a crime without everyone immediately knowing that he's planning to do it. An even stranger twist is in Poul Anderson's *Brain Wave* (1954) where for millions of years the Earth has been passing through a cosmic cloud that was repressing the intelligence of every living creature. When the Earth leaves the influence of the cloud, the intelligence of every living thing is suddenly increased, so that animals become as intelligent as humans, while humans become superintelligent.

Superchildren living in the midst of "normal" humans is the theme of a number of novels including Alexander Key's *Escape to Witch Mountain* (1968), Timothy Zahn's *A Coming of Age* (1985), and Carole Nelson Douglas's *Probe* (1986).

Cyberpunk

The newest form of science fiction (though its roots lie in earlier books by writers Alfred Bester and Philip K. Dick), cyberpunk (a term coined by Gardner Dozois in the mid-1980s) mixes the world of computers and high technology with a countercultural denial of traditional values. Like the punk music from which its name is borrowed, cyberpunk is fast-paced, surprising, anarchistic, and very political or antipolitical, as the case may be. Most cyberpunk novels are filled with dazzling layers of densely described detail. Much of their speculative future is bleak, violent, and oppressive, like the future depicted in the film *Blade Runner*, which had considerable impact on cyberpunk writers. The writer most identified with cyberpunk is William Gibson. His hero in the novel *Neuromancer* (1984)—is able to enter the world of "cyberspace," a word he coined himself. Other writers who have made a name in cyberpunk are Bruce Sterling and Rudy Rucker, a professional mathematician.

In 1990, William Gibson and Bruce Sterling managed a difficult task to combine three entirely different varieties of science fiction into one book, *The Difference Engine*. First, the novel is very cyberpunk. A giant supercomputer controls every aspect of human life but does not do its work very well. The computer in question is an enormous device

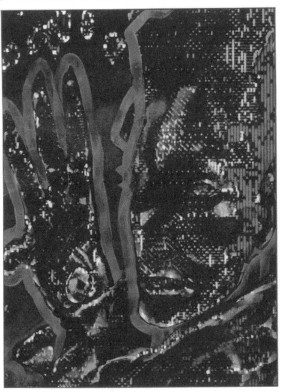

**THE BOOK OF THE YEAR!
WINNER OF THE HUGO, NEBULA AND
PHILIP K. DICK AWARDS!**

NEUROMANCER
WILLIAM GIBSON

ACE • 0-441-56959-5 • [$5.99 CANADA] • **$4.99 U.S.**

*"KALEIDOSCOPIC, PICARESQUE, FLASHY AND DECADENT...AN
AMAZING VIRTUOSO PERFORMANCE...STATE-OF-THE-ART!"*
—WASHINGTON POST

The cover of the paperback edition of William Gibson's *Neuromancer.*

that does all of its calculations mechanically, with gears instead of electronics. It also fits into a very small, little-known category of science fiction called *steampunk*, which are stories that are either set in the nineteenth century or try to imitate the style and feeling of Jules Verne or H.G. Wells. Since *The Difference Engine* is set in the middle of the nineteenth century, it is clearly steampunk. In addition, it is an alternate history since it tries to imagine what the world would be like if computers had been invented a century earlier. *The Difference Engine* is a perfect example of how difficult it can be to divide science fiction into neat categories.

Utopias, Dystopias, and the End of the World

The word *utopia* is used to describe any ideal, perfect society. Although first used by Sir Thomas More in his book *Utopia* (1516), utopias had been the subject of many earlier stories. Most utopian books are not very good because their authors are usually much more interested in demonstrating their own personal ideas about society than in telling a good story. Perhaps the most famous is Plato's account of Atlantis, which he described so well that many people believed it really existed. There have been countless utopias: where scientists run everything, where it is totally communistic, where everything is totally capitalistic, or run entirely by women, where there is no government at all, and so on. These societies all run like clockwork, and all of their citizens are perfectly happy.

Utopias were particularly popular during the nineteenth century because they reflected the time's increasing concern with social issues. It was a century of great political and social revolution, and just about everyone had his own idea about how the world should be run.

Jules Verne tried his hand at creating utopian stories, though the

A map of the Island of Utopia and its alphabet from Sir Thomas More's *Utopia*

results were far from his best books. He wrote about the United States a thousand years in the future in the short novel *In the Year 2889* (1889), and he created one of the more unusual utopias in *The Floating Island* (1895)—a floating city four and a half miles long and three miles wide.

H.G. Wells, with his great interest in social reform, found the utopian story an ideal outlet for his ideas. In *When the Sleeper Wakes* (1899), Wells describes a future city filled with technological and scientific marvels, all managed by the kind of socialist government he championed.

Somewhat more readable than most utopias are the *dystopias*. The opposite of the utopias, the dystopias describe societies where everything has gone wrong. The most famous of these is probably George Orwell's *1984* (1949), in which he describes a world run by a dictator known only as Big Brother, where there is neither personal freedom nor privacy. Dystopias take place in a *post-apocalyptic* future, a future after some great catastrophe—usually an atomic war— and the surviving members of humanity are driven to a primitive struggle for existence. Walter M. Miller Jr.'s novel *A Canticle for Leibowitz* (1960) talks about a postwar future in which science has been virtually forgotten, and ancient textbooks are mistaken for religious relics. Many films of this type have been made: *Mad Max, Waterworld,* and *Terminator* are good examples.

Sir Arthur C. Clarke wrote his own dystopia in *Against the Fall of Night* (1948), where in the far distant future boredom reigns supreme and all ambition has died. Most of the city's people spend their lives engaging in great adventures—plugged into virtual reality machines from the safety of their own homes.

Speculating on how the world may end has always been a favorite theme of science fiction. Just how complete the destruction is depends on how each author defines the word *world*. Some are satisfied with just wiping out the human race—as Wells nearly did in *The War of the Worlds*—while others aren't happy with anything less than the destruction of the Earth itself. *When Worlds Collide* (1932) by Philip Wylie and Edwin Balmer was one of the first and best end-of-the-world novels. Two stray planets wander into our solar system, one of them on a collision course with Earth. With enough time to build a handful of spaceships before the collision, a few hundred people are able to make the transfer to the second new world. Forty-five years later, Larry Niven and Jerry Pournelle wrote a spectacularly realistic story about a comet striking Earth and its aftermath in *Lucifer's Hammer* (1977).

Extraterrestrials

Aliens are as much a part of the popular image of science fiction as spaceships. The first *extraterrestrials* appeared in fiction almost as soon as it was discovered that there were other worlds. Until the end of the nineteenth century, most aliens were assumed to be more or less human-like, regardless of the planet they were from. Only very few authors stopped to consider that environments different from those on Earth might evolve different creatures.

For the most part, alien beings were not considered threatening to Earth until H.G. Wells wrote *The War of the Worlds* (1898). Wells's book introduced the idea of war-like aliens invading our planet, from which thematically came countless science fiction stories. But the aliens in these stories, regardless of how bizarre they looked physically, were still basically human in their motivations and thought processes. It was as though most science fiction aliens were just people wearing monster costumes. Eventually the public accepted aliens to be this way, and they developed into science fiction stereotypes. However, that stereotype began to change with the publication of Stanley Weinbaum's "A Martian Odyssey" (1934), which introduced the concept that a truly alien creature would have a truly alien, nonhuman mind with thought processes and motivations that humans might not understand. An alien might be neither good nor evil . . . just *alien*. Isaac Asimov described Weinbaum's accomplishment:

> *"The pre-Weinbaum extraterrestrial, whether humanoid or monstrous, served only to impinge upon the hero, to serve as a menace or a means of rescue, to be evil or good in strictly human terms—never to be something in itself, independent of mankind.*
>
> *Weinbaum was the first, as far as I know, to create extraterrestrials that had their own reasons for existing."*

Although many other authors followed Weinbaum's example and created truly alien biologies and cultures, most science fiction aliens followed the stereotypes of alien-as-villain or alien-as-human-in-monster-costume well into the 1950s. Then Hal Clement published *Mission of Gravity* (1954), the first of a whole series of books featuring well-thought-out aliens. His extraterrestrials were both physical and mental products of their alien environments. Since then, a number of authors have featured—and specialized in—realistic alien beings. Larry Niven's novels, for example *Ringworld* (1970), *The World of Ptavvs* (1966), *Neutron Star* (1968), and *The Mote in God's Eye* (1974, with Jerry Pournelle), are filled with extraordinary and believable creatures.

The potential difficulty of being able to recognize alien life or intelligence has been the theme of many stories. Alien life might be so very

The cover illustration by H. W. Wesso for *Astounding Stories* in October 1931. The planetary explorers attempt to disintegrate the Rogans, the name for the aliens in the story "The Red Hell of Jupiter."

different that we might not recognize it if we saw it. Even if we did, its intelligence might be so very different from ours that we might not be able to communicate.

Several authors have considered what the consequences of the first human contact with an alien race might be for either species. The first story that looked at the problem seriously was probably Murry Leinster's "First Contact" (1945), which also lent its name to this type of event. When *Star Trek* based a movie on the first meeting of human beings with extraterrestrials, it borrowed the phrase "first contact" as part of the film's title. While most pulp magazine-type stories and novels dwelled upon alien invasion of Earth and interplanetary war, some authors were considerably more thoughtful, wondering what one might realistically expect should human beings ever confront an intelligent alien race. There have, of course, been as many answers to that question as there have been authors. These have ranged in extremes from where Earth is literally quarantined and off-limits to the rest of the universe to where aliens are able to live peacefully alongside human beings.

The theme of alien-human contact is one of the most powerful of all those explored in science fiction. Writers have not yet tired of it, nor have they come close to examining all of its possibilities. In contrast to the early years of science fiction when so many aliens wanted to take over Earth, aliens today seem to be friendlier toward the possibility of human-alien confrontation; any meeting would be civilized and amicable. Two perfect examples of this are Steven Spielberg's film *Close Encounters of the Third Kind* (1977) and Roger Zemeckis's film *Contact* (1997), based on Carl Sagan's book of the same title, in which contact with aliens is discovered to be spiritually uplifting. Such optimism, while commendable, fails to take into account what has hap-

The scene from *Close Encounters of the Third Kind* when the alien mother ship arrives to meet the humans

pened historically on Earth when a technologically superior, or at least more aggressive, culture confronts a more primitive one.

Religion

Although there have been numerous science fiction novels concerning or involving religion, the relationship between the two has always been uneasy. At first glance one might think that science fiction, with its emphasis on rationality, would be the last place to find stories with religious themes. But many writers have found it to be an ideal outlet for their thoughts and beliefs.

Science fiction can explore religion in several different ways and often better than any other form of fiction. It can describe the effects of religion on societies and individuals, how religious beliefs are tested by reality, and the experience of religious transcendence—the pure "sense of wonder" that is the essence of science fiction and immeasurable by science.

Science fiction's ability to ask "what if?" has allowed writers to use religious themes in the creation of other worlds or for those in the future. In Ray Bradbury's "The Fire Balloons" (1951), he asks "what if" there was an alien race that had never fallen from grace and never knew original sin? Or in his story "The Man" (1949), he asks "what if" Jesus had walked on worlds other than this one? In Arthur C. Clarke's story "The Star" (1955), he asks what it might mean if we learned that the Star of Bethlehem had been a nova that had wiped out an entire civilization when it exploded. In fact, in Michael Moorcock's famous novel *Behold the Man* (1969), a time traveler goes back in search of Jesus and eventually becomes the man he is looking for.

Chapter Six
Science Fiction on the Screen

The Movies

Science fiction and movies were made for each other. When the motion picture was invented at the end of the nineteenth century, it actually seemed like something straight out of science fiction. Even to an age accustomed to miracles like the telephone, phonograph, steam engine, and electric light, seeing pictures come to life was astonishing. Although the longest silent film shown at the turn of the nineteenth century was only a few minutes, motion pictures were incredibly popular. People would stand in line for the thrill of seeing ordinary subjects—speeding locomotives, horse-and-buggies, coaches in the streets, dancers, even people sneezing—made extraordinary by the illusion of reality.

Few of these films told a story; it seemed enough just to see the silent images move on film. However, it was not long before someone tried to tell a story, and many of these very first movies were science fiction. The first ones were made by a stage magician named Georges Méliès. He made a specialty of fantastic films and adapted several from Jules Verne novels. The most famous of these early films was *A Trip to the Moon*, created in 1902. Méliès used every trick he knew to make a movie fun to watch. The first science fiction movie to actually tell a real story was

A Trip to the Moon (1902) by Georges Méliès was one of the very first science fiction films. It has been rumored that Jules Verne himself visited the set while it was being shot.

probably *The Airship Destroyer* (1909) by Charles Urban, barely twenty minutes long. Inventor Thomas Edison made a version of *Frankenstein* in 1910. It was hand-colored like many of Méliès's films and borrowed many of the Frenchman's tricks.

In spite of the pioneering work of French and American filmmakers, many of the best science fiction films made during the silent era were German. Films such as *The Golem* (1914) and *Metropolis* (1927) set such very high standards for storytelling, special effects, photography, and acting that American films were influenced by them for many future decades. *Metropolis,* directed by Fritz Lang, is such a good film that it's still being shown today. Fritz Lang also made *Woman in the Moon* (1928), the first serious film about a trip into space. In order to make his cinematic space flight as realistic as possible, Lang recruited Hermann Oberth, one of the world's greatest experts in rockets. Oberth designed the movie rocket and made sure that all of the scientific details were accurate. Unfortunately, once his astronauts reached the moon, Lang threw aside all "real" science by having them discover a breathable atmosphere, among other things. Still, the movie established new standards for the realism of special effects and made one small contribution to the history of space travel: the countdown.

In the United States, filmmakers were taking a more commercial approach to science fiction, emphasizing adventure and thrills over content, story, and character. In 1925 there was a film adaptation of Sir Arthur Conan Doyle's novel *The Lost World,* which was about the discovery of living dinosaurs on a remote plateau in South America. After some exciting adventures, his explorers manage to bring a living dinosaur back to London, where it escapes and causes considerable havoc before swimming out to sea, presumably trying to find its way back to Venezuela. The film's animated dinosaurs, created by Willis O'Brien, were accomplished so

Various scenes from the film *The Lost World* (1925), based on the novel by Arthur Conan Doyle

realistically that Doyle was able to show clips from the film to a famous scientific society, fooling them into believing that they were seeing footage of authentic dinosaurs! O'Brien later perfected his animation techniques in such classic films as *King Kong* (1933) and *Mighty Joe Young* (1949).

Two of the most memorable and important science fiction films made in Britian were based on books by H.G. Wells: *The Invisible Man*

(1933) and *Things to Come* (1936), which Wells himself wrote especially for the screen. *Things to Come* was the first epic science fiction to be made in English. Even though it is a talkative, didactic film, it made an enormous impact on science fiction and is still impressive to watch today. Unfortunately, much of this impact was lost on American filmmakers, who responded with their own version, which became a dreadful musical comedy called *Just Imagine.* The only thing memorable about the American film (which takes place in the far future of 1980!) is its spaceship, a beautiful art deco creation that was later immortalized when it was reused in the Flash Gordon film serials (1936–40).

The first serious science fiction film made after World War II—and the first serious film about space flight since *Woman in the Moon*—was *Destination Moon,* produced by George Pal in 1950. Filmed in a realistic, documentary style, the story is simply about the first trip to the moon. Made in color with Academy Award-winning special effects and co-written by science fiction author Robert A. Heinlein, the movie had a true-to-life reality that is convincing even today.

Instead of capitalizing on the success of *Destination Moon* by making more and better science fiction films, 1950s Hollywood produced more movies about monsters, giant ants, octopi, scorpions, and other mutated animals. If space flight was even mentioned, it was usually as an excuse to introduce some alien horror.

Some science fiction films of the 1950s were influenced by Cold War concerns about the atomic bomb. They approached this subject in two ways: the effects of nuclear radiation and warnings about nuclear war. The former was most often expressed as mutated people and animals. The best of these included films such as *Them!,* in which giant ants invade Los Angeles, and the worst included films like *The Amazing Colossal Man,* whose title says it all. Warnings about the misuse of atomic power usually came from aliens, who visited Earth to either stop us or guide us. Probably the most notable of these was *The Day the Earth Stood Still.* After a flying saucer lands on the White House lawn, its passenger offers the nations of the world a frightening ultimatum: abandon nuclear warfare or the aliens will destroy Earth.

Fears about the United States being taken over by a totalitarian government inspired *Invasion of the Body Snatchers* (1956, remade 1978), one of the scariest films ever made. Its story of strange pods that create emotionless duplicates of human beings has an underlying theme of the loss of individual identity.

Perhaps the best science fiction film to come out of the 1950s—and still one of the best science fiction films ever made—was *Forbidden Planet* (1956). The first big-budget science fiction film to be released by a major studio, *Forbidden Planet* was a top-notch production. Based loosely on Shakespeare's *The Tempest,* the movie was intelligent, well written, well acted, and boasts spectacular special effects. It also introduced Robby the Robot, one of science fiction's most enduring icons. Later, *Forbidden Planet* was also one of the inspirations for perhaps the greatest of all science fiction film and television phenomena: *Star Trek.*

The good films produced during this period stand above their competition. Perhaps part of the reason for their success came from the fact that they were based on good science fiction stories and novels. The best of these was made by people who respected science fiction. *The Day the Earth Stood Still* (1951) was based on the story "Farewell to the Master" (1940) by Harry Bates; *The Thing from Another World* (1951) came from "Who Goes There?" by John W. Campbell Jr.; *It Came from Outer Space* (1953) was written in part by Ray Bradbury; *This Island Earth* (1955) was taken from the 1952 novel by Raymond Jones; *The War of the Worlds*

(1953) was based on the H.G. Wells novel; and *The Incredible Shrinking Man* (1956) came from the novel by Richard Matheson. All of these movies are still worth watching. Like the best of written science fiction, these films use science fiction to explore ideas and issues as well as understand people more clearly.

There were fewer science fiction films made during the 1960s, but those few are memorable. With its convincing special effects, realistic sets, and scrupulous attention to scientific and medical detail, *Fantastic Voyage* (1966) convinced everyone that its premise could really happen. The crew and its submarine are shrunk to microscopic size so that they can be injected into a human body in order to perform a delicate brain operation from the inside. In the same year François Truffaut's adaptation of Ray Bradbury's novel *Fahrenheit 451* was released. *Planet of the Apes,* an adaptation of the Pierre Boule novel, was the big science fiction film of 1968. But the biggest and most important science fiction film of the decade—and perhaps of all time—was Stanley Kubrick's *2001: A Space Odyssey.* Afterward, science fiction movies were never the same. Even though Hollywood continued to produce the same alien-as-enemy films, all were severely influenced by the sophisticated special effects of *2001.* Also, *2001* demonstrated that there was an audience for intelligent, thoughtful, literate science fiction films. Gradually, more of them began to appear, but to this day they are still in the minority.

The most popular science fiction films of the last decades of the twentieth century were those of the *Star Wars* series. A throwback to the pulp fiction and the old Flash Gordon serials of the 1930s, the *Star Wars* series was much more science fantasy than science fiction; indeed, scientific ideas and concepts play little or no part in *Star Wars.* These movies are equivalent to the planet-busting space operas of E.E. Smith.

The promotional poster for the film *Forbidden Planet* (1956) depicts Robby the Robot carrying Altaira, the daughter of Doctor Morbius, the robot's creator.

Recent films have been heavily influenced by the cyberpunk sub-genre of science fiction novels, which concern themselves with human-computer interactivity. The earliest of these may have been Disney's *Tron* (1982), and a recent example was *The Matrix* (1999).

R2-D2 and C-3PO from the *Star Wars* series. Although called "droids" in the films, they are actually robots.

Television

If science fiction has generally fared badly at the hands of Hollywood, it has done far worse on television. For most of the first thirty years of television, science fiction was reduced to cheaply produced children's programming, such as *Space Patrol, Tom Corbett,* or *Captain Video*, which were only slightly better than the *Flash Gordon* serials. Still, many of these early series are fondly remembered by those who watched them; they certainly inspired more than one aerospace career. Though excruciatingly primitive by today's standards—most of them were broadcast live and had budgets of only a few hundred dollars—they did manage to instill a sense of wonder about the universe and a positive, optimistic outlook about the future of science and space travel. On the other hand, the 1960s television series *The Twilight Zone* and especially *The Outer Limits* explored many important science fiction themes. Many of their stories were either taken from or written by some of the best science fiction authors in the business.

However, it wasn't until the advent of *Star Trek* that science fiction on television really took off. For millions of people who had thought of science fiction as only "that Buck Rogers stuff," Gene Roddenberry's *Star Trek* was a revelation. Although the original series was short-lived—it only lasted three seasons (seventy-nine episodes)—it eventually spawned an even more successful series of motion pictures as well as three popular spin-off television series: *Star Trek: The Next Generation*, *Star Trek: Deep Space 9,* and *Star Trek: Voyager*. One important aspect of the *Star Trek* series that sets it apart from most other television science fiction is the attention it pays to human problems. Through characters such as the android Data or the biomechanical Seven of Nine, it can deal with such metaphysical concepts as the nature of what it means to be "human." The science in *Star Trek*—particularly in the later series—is consistently good, too, with a number of experts advising the writers so that scientific mistakes are avoided.

Science fiction has fared less well with other popular series, such as *Battlestar Galactica* and *Babylon 5*, which concentrate on *Star Wars*-like intergalactic warfare to the exclusion of any concepts derived from science or any special concern with human issues. They are old-fashioned space operas straight from the pages of *Amazing Stories*.

One of the most popular science fiction series in recent years is

Captain Kirk (William Shatner), Spock (Leonard Nimoy), and Dr. McCoy (DeForest Kelley) from the first *Star Trek* series in a scene from "The Apple"

The X Files, which in some ways is very antiscience. If it doesn't treat most scientists as outright villains, it at least suggests that they can't be trusted. The show consistently deals with subjects that are usually thought of as pseudoscience or superstition: ESP, aliens and UFOs, the Bermuda Triangle, vampires, astrology, and so forth.

Chapter Seven
Science Fiction Art

More than any other form of literature, science fiction is defined by its images, and many of its artists are as famous as its authors. Most science fiction fans can tell you the names of their favorite artists as easily as they can list their favorite authors. Very often the illustrations that science fiction artists create can stand alone from the books and magazines for which they were painted.

Science fiction art has its own history, and in some ways it is a history independent from science fiction literature. From the beginning of time artists have enjoyed depicting fantastic adventures, weird creatures, and strange places. Sometimes they did this for their own pleasure, to amaze or frighten their viewers, and to illustrate religious or mythological ideas.

As long ago as the fifteenth century, artists like Hieronymus Bosch (1450–1516) and Pieter Bruegel the Younger (1564–1638) created nightmarish paintings and drawings, some of them filled with literally hundreds of monsters and demons.

Just as there were few writers who specialized in writing science fiction until the middle of the nineteenth century, there were few artists who could be rightly called "science fiction artists." Oddly enough, the first two science fiction artists didn't illustrate someone else's novels or stories. In fact, they seldomly illustrated any stories at all. Rather, they let their work stand on its own. In 1844 and 1847 a French artist named Ignace-Isidore Gérard (1830–1847)—who worked under the name of Isidore Grandville—published two collections of drawings: *Un Autre Monde* (Another World) and *Les Fleurs Animées* (Living Flowers). These books were filled with incredible monsters, weird creatures, and fantastic machines, all of which might have come from a science fiction pulp magazine of the 1930s or 40s. Another French artist, Albert Robida (1848–1926), was much more seriously interested in science and invention, and his artwork is much less fantasy-oriented than Grandville's. Robida's illustrations foresaw many of the horrors of mechanized warfare—including the use of aircraft—as well as many modern inventions, such as television.

In the United States, many famous illustrators were called upon to create artwork for science fiction stories. N.C. Wyeth, (1882–1945) for example—the father of Andrew Wyeth (b. 1917) and grandfather of Jamie Wyeth (b. 1946)—illustrated Jules Verne's *Mysterious Island*.

With the advent of the pulp magazines, there also came a need for artists to create hundreds of covers and interior illustrations. These artists got paid less than the writers but continued because they were very good and genuinely enjoyed their work.

The first great name in science fiction art was an Austrian immigrant named Frank R. Paul (1884–1963). Almost single-handedly,

Grandville's "The Peregrinations of a Comet" from his collection *Un Autre Monde* (1847)

A 1918 illustration by N.C. Wyeth from *The Mysterious Island* by Jules Verne

Paul created science fiction art as a special field to itself. Trained as an architect, he was working as a newspaper illustrator when Hugo Gernsback gave him a job illustrating for his science magazines. He did virtually every cover and all of the interior drawings for these magazines. He was a master at creating fantastic architecture and machines. No matter how incredible, Paul's illustrations looked as though they might work. While his paintings seem almost crude today, with their bold colors and stiffly drawn people, they are enormously influential. Many science fiction artists even now are inspired by Paul's exciting vision of the future.

There were other artists who not only made a name for themselves in the science fiction pulps but whose work contributed something to the evolution and growth of science fiction art. Leo Morey took over much of Paul's work when Gernsback lost control of *Amazing Stories*. As an artist he was much better than Paul; while his futuristic cities and machines were not as well thought-out as his predecessor's, the quality of his illustrations was much higher. An even greater improvement was made by Howard V. Brown who worked for *Astounding Stories*. Brown could draw and paint expertly, and his machines and aliens were startlingly realistic.

Science fiction art changed just as science fiction writing changed when editor John W. Campbell Jr. took over *Astounding Stories* in 1937. Campbell insisted on less garish, less sensational, more sedate, and more thoughtful cover art. Campbell wanted the covers of his magazine to look as literary as the contents were. He was not always successful in this, as he admitted, because he knew almost nothing about art.

Among the artists Campbell recruited were Earle K. Bergey, one of the most skilled artists to ever work for the pulp magazines, and Alex

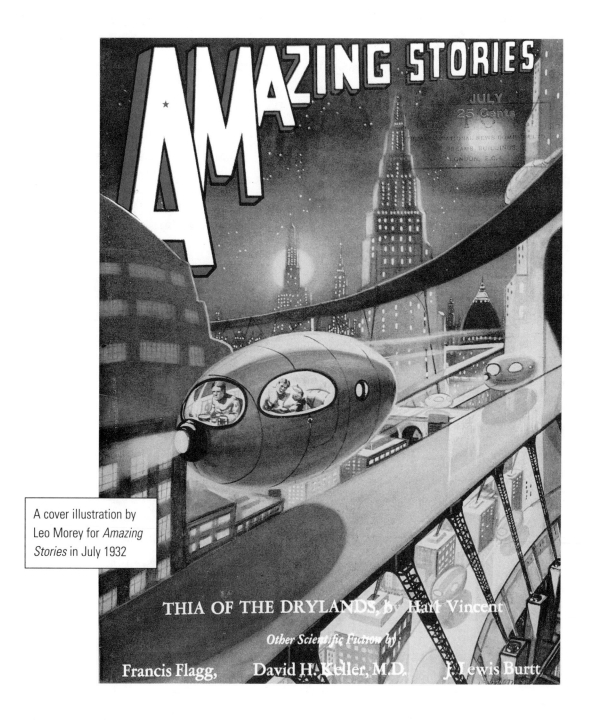

A cover illustration by Leo Morey for *Amazing Stories* in July 1932

Schomburg, who was a master of the air brush. Another artist was Hubert Rogers, who provided some of the greatest science fiction magazine covers ever published for *Astounding Stories*. He was a superb figure painter; the characters looked like real people. He also introduced the idea of illustrating his subjects symbolically. Rogers brought a new sophistication and intelligence to science fiction art.

A number of artists preferred to work in pen and ink, specializing in creating interior artwork. Among these were Paul Orban, Stephen Lawrence, Elliott Dold, and Virgil Finlay. Of these, the most famous was Finlay, who received in 1953 the first Hugo Award for art, the science fiction equivalent of the Academy Award, and whose work is still admired and collected today, many years after his death.

Comic books and comic strips have always been a part of the story of science fiction art. One of the first science fiction comics was *Buck Rogers*. Its popularity spawned a twelve-part serial in 1939, which provided inspiration for the 1970s television series. Unfortunately, *Buck Rogers* may have been *too* popular. For most non–science fiction readers, it became synonymous with science fiction, and the exclamation "It's like something out of *Buck Rogers*!" proliferated. As much fun as *Buck Rogers* was, it still represented some of the most juvenile and even old-fashioned aspects of science fiction. It certainly wasn't representative of the stories and novels being published at the same time. It took science fiction many decades, probably well into the 1960s, to finally shake this image.

Only in the last few years have comic books begun to approach the quality and influence of the written word, mostly with the development of the *graphic novel*, an idea imported from Europe. With their often extraordinary artwork, creative design, and sophisticated stories (sometimes written by science fiction authors themselves), graphic novels have become a legitimate and exciting form of science fiction.

A newspaper page of the science fiction comic strip *Buck Rogers* in 1932. Artwork by Dick Calkins

After World War II, the boom in paperback publishing created many changes in science fiction illustration. The covers of the first paperback science fiction books resembled the pulp magazines, but they soon took on a look of their own. Few pulp artists were able to make the move to the paperbacks. One of the best of these artists was Frank Kelly Freas (b. 1922). Freas's work has been enormously diverse, running the gamut from almost cartoon-like space opera to the most subtle, sensitive concepts. Winning the Hugo Award for best artist more often than anyone else, he began his career working for pulps such as *Weird Tales* and *Astounding Stories*, and is still working today for paperbacks. His work has also appeared in books, as posters, and on rock album covers.

There is no single artistic style or technique that can be singled out as being science fiction. But there are many different styles, and to list them would be as impossible as it would be to list all the different science fiction writers. Some artists, though, have specialized in certain styles: Boris Vallejo (b. 1941) and his wife Julie Bell have made a specialty of heroic fantasy; Bob Eggleton (b. 1960) is best at alien worlds; Stephen Hickman (b. 1949) is as good at fantasy as he is at creating alien creatures and amazing spacecraft; Vincent Di Fate (b. 1945) is a master of futuristic hardware; and Michael Whelan (b. 1950), equally adept at painting every subject of science fiction and fantasy, is perhaps the finest of the modern science fiction artists. Science fiction art has never been better. Some of the finest illustrators in the world are creating science fiction art, and some of the finest covers being published anywhere are on science fiction books.

Just as science fiction authors specialize in different ideas of science fiction, the artists, too, specialize in different subjects. Some are at their best creating the hardware of science fiction, while others specialize in aliens, action scenes, fantasy, or symbolism.

The pioneer artist who specialized in depicting scenes of other planets and alien worlds was Chesley Bonestell (1888-1986). He created astonishingly realistic scenes set on other planets. Considered a serious and important artist even outside the field of science fiction, Bonestell set a new level for craftsmanship and quality in science fiction art. The paintings he did for a series of articles in the early 1950s about the future of space flight, written for *Collier's* magazine by space expert Wernher von Braun, are credited with helping inspire the United State's fledgling space program.

Another specialty of science fiction illustration is *gadget* or *hardware painting*. There are artists who specialize in creating fantastic machines, inventions, and spacecraft. One of the very best of these artists is Robert McCall (b. 1919), who is probably most famous for his paintings advertising *2001: A Space Odyssey*. He has also worked in motion pictures, creating spaceships for Disney's *The Black Hole* (1979), and he has painted many space-themed murals such as the one in the entrance to the National Air & Space Museum in Washington, D.C. While Syd Mead's art has seldom if ever appeared on a science fiction book cover, his art has been enormously influential because of the designs he created for the movies *Blade Runner, 2010* (1984), and *Aliens* (1986).

Artists whose names have been most closely associated with the illustration of alien life-forms are Edd Cartier (b. 1914), John Schoenherr (b. 1935), and Wayne Barlowe (b. 1958). Although Cartier did a few color paintings, he is best known for his black-and-white interior drawings for the magazines *Unknown* and *Planet Stories*. Schoenherr is one of the world's most respected wildlife painters, and is best known for having created the original illustrations for the science fiction classic *Dune*. Barlowe is the youngest of the three and the only one who has made a genuine specialty of creating alien creatures. He has even published an award-winning book, *Barlowe's Guide to Extraterrestrials*, in which he depicts virtually all of the most important aliens in science fiction literature.

An alien lifeform by Wayne Barlowe

Chapter Eight

Science Fiction and Real Life

I t's hard to believe that science fiction was once considered third-class writing, suitable only for children or for adults who didn't want to read "good" literature. Today, with college courses in science fiction and even books like this one, no one sneers at science fiction any longer. Few people consider it less literary than any other genre. In fact, because of its lack of limitations or boundaries—or even rules, for that matter—there have been more science fiction books accepted as good literature than in any other category of fiction. This is in large part because the best science fiction is always about human beings.

Science Fiction As Prophecy

Much has been debated about science fiction's ability to predict the future. At first glance, there seems to be some truth to this theory. After all, didn't science fiction authors write about space travel, television, and computers long before such things were made?

Very few science fiction authors have ever set out to accurately predict future events or technology. If an attempt were made, the results were terrible: bad fiction and bad prophecies. A successful example, though, is Hugo Gernsback's "Ralph 124C41+." The story is famous for having a detailed description of radar almost thirty years before it was actually developed—and it even included a diagram!

There are several ways in which a science fiction book can seem prophetic (and examples of almost all can be found in "Ralph"). First, an author takes everyday things and simply makes them bigger, smaller, or faster—in some way more "perfect." This kind of prophesy is the easiest to make and might be called the "wishful thinking" prophesy. In "Ralph," when Gernsback wrote about "non-rusting steel," did he really predict stainless steel, or was he just making a wishful "improvement" on ordinary steel?

Second, some prophecies exist only in the reader's mind. This usually happens when a vague description sounds familiar and the reader jumps to the conclusion that the author made a prediction. A good example of this is found in "Ralph." Gernsback describes a lighting fixture as looking like a glowing coil, and some people have jumped to the conclusion that Gernsback predicted neon signs. Since Gernsback didn't add any further description as to how his lights actually worked, he didn't really predict anything.

Third, a prophecy might be the result of parallel evolution. When a science fiction author in the past described a detailed space suit, a planetary landing, or some electronic device, and years later the description reads exactly like the actual thing, the truth is that most likely the author first introduced the idea and then future scientists just carried it to fruition. Most of these prophecies are just logical extensions of contemporary science. So many authors are working scientists, inventors, teachers, or engineers and can easily see where technology is heading.

A good example can be found in Jules Verne's *From the Earth to the Moon*. Many people are still amazed to discover that he set his launch site in central Florida, only a few miles from where the Kennedy Space Center was eventually located and the Apollo lunar landings launched. But the reason Verne placed his giant gun in Florida was that he wanted a location in the United States nearest the equator and the least distant from the moon—exactly the same reason NASA had. Prophetic? No. It was just two similar solutions for the same problem.

Fourth, an author can cause his own prophecy to come true. This is called a self-fulfilling prophecy. Again, Jules Verne is an excellent example. His book *From the Earth to the Moon* inspired many scientists to invent space travel, including those who were most responsible for starting modern space flight. Did he then predict space travel or did he cause it to happen? A little of both.

Still, in spite of all this, some science fiction writers had an uncanny window into the future. For example, most authors up until the early 1960s underestimated the wide future use of computers. This was understandable since most of the early computers were enormous machines. In the 1940s and early 1950s, a computer not much more powerful than an average desktop computer today would literally fill an entire building. This was mainly because the first computers relied on vacuum tubes: no one was able to predict the invention of the transistor and the other solid-state electronics that made small, powerful computers possible.

Two stories in particular seem even more remarkable for their prescience. The first story is "A Logic Named Joe" (1946) by Will F. Jenkins. Written at a time when the smallest electronic computers were not only enormous in size but also cost many millions of dollars, the story takes place in the near future when every home has a small, desktop computer. Jenkins describes this as looking like a television screen with a keyboard attached. These computers are hooked up to larger, central computers that are in turn hooked up to giant mainframes. People use their personal computers for all sorts of things that sound very familiar today: keeping household records, writing letters, doing research, getting news and stock market quotes, making video phone calls. In other words, Jenkins described the Internet in perfect detail. But being a good science fiction writer, he went further and described the impact this might have on society, in particular the indiscriminate availability of any and all information to whoever wanted it, even if that information might prove to be dangerous.

Isaac Asimov looked at the possibility of miniaturized personal computers from a different angle in "The Feeling of Power" (1959). At that time, there was no such thing as a personal computer, let alone hand-held calculators. The only thing that mathematicians and students had to work with was a mechanical device, usually made of wood and/or plastic, called a slide rule. But Asimov described powerful, pocket-sized computers had been used by everyone for years. They had been used for so long, in fact, that no one even remembers that it's possible to do calculations on paper. When a technician rediscovers the art of doing math by hand, no one believes him. In fact, they consider him to be either mad or a dangerous radical. But the word gets out and others start to rediscover mathematics:

> "Nine times seven, thought Shuman with deep satisfaction, is sixty-three, and I don't need a computer to tell me so. The computer is in my own head.
>
> And it was amazing the feeling of power that gave him."

Science Fiction Fans

From the very beginning, science fiction has attracted a special group of admirers. In fact, science fiction was probably the first category of fiction to have developed its own group of fans. These fans (*fandom* in their language) have been a powerful influence in the development of science fiction.

One of the most popular features of the first science fiction magazines was the letter column, where enthusiastic readers could comment on stories, their favorite authors and artists, or almost any other subject they cared to discuss. Sometimes debates between readers would fill the letter column pages for many issues. Some of these early fans became science fiction authors. Going through the old magazines of the 1930s, 40s, 50s, and 60s, one can find teenage letters from people who later became some of the biggest names in science fiction.

It wasn't long before the fans wanted to actually meet one another and formed dozens of clubs. The first science fiction convention was held in Philadelphia, Pennsylvania, in 1937. It was just a meeting of a handful of fans from that city and nearby New York. In 1939 the first "world science fiction convention" took place in New York. Two hundred fans attended. Today, a world science fiction convention can attract ten thousand people.

There are dozens of science fiction conventions (called "cons") every year. Most of these are small, regional conventions, usually attracting just a few hundred fans from a small area. Typically, a convention features a "huckster's room" where books, magazines, and other science fiction items are sold and traded. Larger conventions will have special speakers, at least one guest of honor, usually a well-known author or editor, masquerades, a banquet, and other events. Almost all conventions will have an art show. Many professional writers, editors, and artists will attend on their own since they are usually fans, too. The big world conventions, which are held in a different city every year, are so large and so important that major motion pictures will sometimes premier at them. Most science fiction magazines will list the dates and locations of upcoming conventions. A bookstore will also be likely to help you find a local science fiction club.

Fans indulge in many other activities in addition to holding meetings and organizing conventions. Many clubs and individuals publish

Two *Babylon 5* fans are dressed as Delenn and G'Kar at a convention.

fanzines, which are short for fan magazines. Some of these are just a few pages copied as cheaply as possible and stapled together, while others are professionally printed and look like the professional magazines (or prozines in fan talk). They publish news, opinions, reviews, stories, and poetry. Many professional writers got their start publishing or writing for fanzines. Lois McMaster Bujold, one of today's best-selling science fiction authors and a three-time Hugo Award winner for best fiction, got her start as a member of a small science fiction club and once published her own *Star Trek* fanzine.

Fandom has in fact been a very important force in the history of science fiction. Dozens upon dozens of authors, editors, publishers, and artists have come from it.

Fans also collect science fiction. They have performed an invaluable service in doing this. Pulp magazines are very fragile and would long ago have disappeared if fans hadn't carefully collected and preserved them. Other fans collect books or artwork. Some fans have donated full collections to major universities where students can admire or research these early histories. Some fans are also serious scholars of science fiction and have written whole books about it.

It is clear that no other form of literature has had such a close relationship with its readers as science fiction.

THE HUGO AND NEBULA AWARDS

The Hugo Awards (named for Hugo Gernsback) are presented every year at the World Science Fiction Convention. The members of the convention, essentially the fans, vote to choose winners in several categories, including best novel, short story, editor, artist, and dramatic presentation. The members of the Science Fiction Writers Association present the Nebula Awards. Together, these awards represent some of the best science fiction written in the last half of the twentieth century.

The first Hugos were given in 1953, while the first Nebulas were awarded in 1965. In the list below, Hugo Awards are designated by an **H**, and Nebulas by an **N**. Only the awards for best novel are listed here.

1953
H: *The Demolished Man*, Alfred Bester

1954

No awards

1955

H: *They'd Rather Be Right*, Mark Clifton and Frank Riley

1956

H: *Double Star*, Robert A. Heinlein

1957

No awards

1958

H: *The Big Time*, Fritz Leiber

1959

H: *A Case of Conscience*, James Blish

1960:

H: *Starship Troopers*, Robert A. Heinlein

1961

H: *A Canticle for Leibowitz*, Walter M. Miller Jr.

1962

H: *Stranger in a Strange Land*, Robert A. Heinlein

1963

H: *The Man in the High Castle*, Philip K. Dick

1964

H: *Way Station*, Clifford D. Simak

1965

H: *The Wanderer*, Fritz Leiber

N: *Dune*, Frank Herbert

1966

H: (tie) *And Call Me Conrad*, Roger Zelazny;
Dune, Frank Herbert

N: (tie) *Flowers for Algernon*, Daniel Keyes;
Babel 17, Samuel R. Delany

1967

H: *The Moon Is a Harsh Mistress*, Robert A. Heinlein

N: *The Einstein Intersection*, Samuel R. Delany

1968

   H: *Lord of Light*, Roger Zelazny

   N: *Rite of Passage*, Alexei Panshin

1969

   H: *Stand on Zanzibar*, John Brunner

   N: *The Left Hand of Darkness*, Ursula K. Le Guin

1970

   H: *The Left Hand of Darkness*, Ursula K. Le Guin

   N: *Ringworld*, Larry Niven

1971

   H: *Ringworld*, Larry Niven

   N: *A Time of Changes*, Robert Silverberg

1972

   H: *To Your Scattered Bodies Go*, Philip José Farmer

   N: *The Gods Themselves*, Isaac Asimov

1973

   H: *The Gods Themselves*, Isaac Asimov

   N: *Rendezvous with Rama*, Arthur C. Clarke

1974

   H: *Rendezvous with Rama*, Arthur C. Clarke

   N: *The Dispossessed*, Ursula K. Le Guin

1975

   H: *The Dispossessed*, Ursula K. Le Guin

   N: *The Forever War*, Joe Haldeman

1976

   H: *The Forever War*, Joe Haldeman

   N: *Man Plus*, Frederik Pohl

1977

   H: *Where Late the Sweet Birds Sang*, Kate Wilhelm

   N: *Gateway*, Frederik Pohl

1978

   H: *Gateway*, Frederik Pohl

   N: *Dreamsnake*, Vonda N. McIntyre

1979

    H: *Dreamsnake*, Vonda N. McIntyre

    N: *The Fountains of Paradise*, Arthur C. Clarke

1980

    H: *The Fountains of Paradise*, Arthur C. Clarke

    N: *Timescape*, Gregory Benford

1981

    H: *The Snow Queen*, Joan Vinge

    N: *The Claw of the Conciliator*, Gene Wolfe

1982

    H: *Downbelow Station*, C.J. Cherryh

    N: *No Enemy But Time*, Michael Bishop

1983

    H: *Foundation's Edge*, Isaac Asimov

    N: *Startide Rising*, David Brin

1984

    H: *Startide Rising*, David Brin

    N: *Neuromancer*, William Gibson

1985

    H: *Neuromancer*, William Gibson

    N: *Ender's Game*, Orson Scott Card

1986

    H: *Ender's Game*, Orson Scott Card

    N: *Speaker for the Dead*, Orson Scott Card

1987

    H: *Speaker for the Dead*, Orson Scott Card

    N: *The Falling Woman*, Pat Murphy

1988

    H: *The Uplift War*, David Brin

    N: *Falling Free*, Lois McMaster Bujold

1989

    H: *Cyteen*, C.J. Cherryh

    N: *The Healer's War*, Elizabeth Ann Scarborough

1990

> **H:** *Hyperion*, Dan Simmons
>
> **N:** *Tehanu*, Ursula K. Le Guin

1991

> **H:** *The Vor Game*, Lois McMaster Bujold
>
> **N:** *Stations of the Tide*, Michael Swanwick

1992

> **H:** *Barrayar*, Lois McMaster Bujold
>
> **N:** *Doomsday Book*, Connie Willis

1993

> **H:** (tie) *A Fire Upon the Deep*, Vernor Vinge;
> *Doomsday Book*, Connie Willis
>
> **N:** *Red Mars*, Kim Stanley Robinson

1994

> **H:** *Green Mars*, Kim Stanley Robinson
>
> **N:** *Moving Mars*, Greg Bear

1995

> **H:** *Mirror Dance*, Lois McMaster Bujold
>
> **N:** (tie) *The Terminal Experiment*, Robert Sawyer;
> *Mother of Storms*, John Barnes

1996

> **H:** *The Diamond Age*, Neal Stephenson
>
> **N:** *Slow River*, Nicola Griffith

1997

> **H:** *Blue Mars*, Kim Stanley Robinson
>
> **N:** *The Moon and the Sun*, Vonda N. McIntyre

1998

> **H:** *The Forever Peace*, Joe Haldeman

1999

> **H:** *A Deepness in the Sky*, Vernor Vinge
>
> **N:** *Parable of the Talents*, Octavia Butler

MORE ABOUT SCIENCE FICTION

For the general history of science fiction, one can hardly do better than James Gunn's *Alternate Worlds* (New York: Prentice-Hall, 1975), David A. Kyle's *A Pictorial History of Science Fiction* (London: Hamlyn Publishing Group, 1976), and Brian Aldiss's *Billion Year Spree* (London: Corgi Books, 1975). Two mammoth encyclopedias of science fiction cover every conceivable topic: *The New Encyclopedia of Science Fiction* (New York: Viking Penguin, 1988) by James Gunn and *The Visual Encyclopedia of Science Fiction* (New York: Harmony Books, 1977) by Brian Ash. Sam Moskowitz has written two collections of biographies of great science fiction authors: *Explorers of the Infinite* (Cleveland: World Publishing Co., 1963) and *Seekers of Tomorrow* (Cleveland: World Publishing Co., 1966). David A. Kyle's *The Illustrated Book of Science Fiction Dreams* (London: Hamlyn Publishing Group, 1977) covers all of the major themes of science fiction while Forrest J. Ackerman's *World of Science Fiction* (Los Angeles: General Publishing Group, 1997) is a fun, general introduction to the subject. Wayne Barlowe's *Barlowe's Guide to Extraterrestrials* (New York: Workman Publishing, 1979) describes many of science fiction's most outstanding alien creatures, and *Firebrands* (London: Paper Tiger, 1998) by Ron Miller and Pamela Sargent is a pictorial guide to science fiction's great female characters. Finally, science fiction illustrator Vincent Di Fate has created the definitive history of science fiction art in *Infinite Worlds* (New York: Penguin Group, 1997).

RECOMMENDED READING

Abbott, Edwin A. *Flatland*. New York: Dover, 1992.

Asimov, Isaac. *Foundation*. New York: Bantam Books, 1991.

————. *Foundation and Empire*. New York: Bantam Books, 1991.

————. *Second Foundation*. New York: Bantam Books, 1991.

————. *I, Robot*. New York: Bantam Books, 1994.

Balmer, Edwin, and Philip Wylie. *When Worlds Collide*. Lincoln: University of Nebraska Press, 1999.

Bradbury, Ray. *Fahrenheit 451*. New York: Ballantine Books, 1996.

————. *The Martian Chronicles*. New York: Bantam Books, 1994.

Card, Orson Scott. *Ender's Game*. New York: Tor Books,1992.

Clarke, Arthur C. *Childhood's End*. New York: Ballantine Books, 1987

————. *A Fall of Moondust*. New York: Bantam Books, 1991.

————. *Rendezvous with Rama*. New York: Bantam Books, 1990.

Du Bois, William Pené. *The 21 Balloons*. New York: Puffin Books, 1986.

Engdahl, Sylvia Louise. *Enchantress from the Stars*. New York: Atheneum, 1970.

Heinlein, Robert A. *Space Cadet*, New York: Ballantine Books, 1992.

————. *The Rolling Stones*. New York: Del Rey, 1985.

————. *The Star Beast*. New York: Ballantine Books, 1995.

————. *Citizen of the Galaxy*. New York: Ballantine Books, 1987.

Henderson, Zenna. *Ingathering*. Boston: NESFA Press, 1995.

Herbert, Frank. *Dune*. New York: Ace Books, 1999.

Huxley, Aldous. *Brave New World*. New York: Harperperennial Library, 1999.

Keyes, Daniel. *Flowers for Algernon*. New York: Bantam Books, 1984.

Le Guin, Ursula K. *The Farthest Shore*. New York: Bantam Books, 1984

————. *The Tombs of Atuan*. New York: Bantam Books, 1984.

————. *The Wizard of Earthsea*. New York: Bantam Books, 1984.

————. *Tehanu*. New York: Bantam Books, 1991.

Leinster, Murray. *First Contacts*. Boston: NESFA Press, 1998.

L'Engle, Madeleine. *A Wrinkle in Time*. New York: Bantam Books, 1981.

————. *A Swiftly-Tilting Planet*. New York: Bantam Books, 1981.

Lewis, C. S. *The Complete Chronicles of Narnia*. New York: HarperCollins, 1994.

McCaffrey, Anne. *Dragonsong*. New York: Bantam Books, 1977.

————. *Dragonsinger*. New York: Bantam Books, 1989.

————. *Dragondrums*. New York: Bantam Books, 1996.

————. *Dragonsdawn*. New York: Bantam Books, 1989.

Niven, Larry. *Ringworld*. New York: Ballantine Books, 1990.

Norton, Andre. *Derelict for Trade*. New York: Tor Books, 1998.

————. *Brother to Shadows*. New York: Avon, 1999.

————. *Songsmith*. New York: Tor Books, 1993.

————. *The Warding of Witch World*. New York: Warner Books, 1998.

O'Brien, Robert C. *Mrs. Frisby and the Rats of NIMH*. New York: Aladdin, 1986.

————. *Z for Zachariah*. New York: Macmillan, 1986.

Paulsen, Gary. *The Transall Saga*. New York: Random House, 1999.

Piper, H. Beam. *The Complete Fuzzy*. NewYork: Ace Books, 1998.

Sargent, Pamela. *Earthseed*. New York: Harper & Row, 1983.

Shelley, Mary Woolstonecraft. *Frankenstein*. New York: Tor Books, 1994.

Smith, E. E. *First Lensman*. Baltimore: Old Earth Books, 1988.

————. *Galactic Patrol*. Baltimore: Old Earth Books, 1998.

————. *Gray Lensman*. Baltimore: Old Earth Books, 1998.

————. *Second Stage Lensman*. Baltimore: Old Earth Books, 1998.

————. *Children of the Lens*. Baltimore: Old Earth Books, 1998.

Stevenson, Robert Louis. *Dr. Jekyll and Mr. Hyde*. New York: Bantam Books, 1982.

Sturgeon, Theodore. *More Than Human*. New York: Vintage, 1999.

Twain, Mark. *A Connecticut Yankee in King Arthur's Court*. New York: NAL, 1990.

Verne, Jules. *A Journey to the Center of the Earth*. London: Oxford University Press, 1998.

————. *From the Earth to the Moon*. New York: Bantam Books, 1993.

————. *20,000 Leagues Under the Sea*. London: Oxford University Press, 1998.

Vinge, Joan. *Psion*. New York: Warner Books, 1996.

Wells, H. G. *The Time Machine*. New York: Tor Books, 1995.

————. *The War of the Worlds*. New York: Tor Books, 1993.

————. *The Invisible Man*. New York: Dover, 1992.

Zebrowski, George. *Sunspacer*. White Wolf, 1998.

RECOMMENDED MOVIES

Metropolis (UFA, 1926)

Frankenstein (Universal, 1931)

King Kong (Universal, 1933)

The Invisible Man (Universal, 1933)

The Bride of Frankenstein (Universal, 1935)

Things to Come (London, 1936)

Destination Moon (Eagle Lion,1950)

The Day the Earth Stood Still (20th Century Fox, 1951)

The Thing (Winchester Pictures, 1951)

The War of the Worlds (Paramount, 1953)

20,000 Leagues Under the Sea (Walt Disney, 1954)

This Island Earth (Universal, 1955)

Forbidden Planet (MGM, 1956)

1984 (Holiday Film Productions., 1956)

Invasion of the Body Snatchers (Walter Wanger, 1956)

The Incredible Shrinking Man (Universal, 1957)

The Time Machine (MGM, 1960)

Fahrenheit 451 (Anglo-Enterprise/Rank/Vinyard, 1966)

Fantastic Voyage (20th Century Fox, 1966)

2001: A Space Odyssey (MGM, 1968)

Sleeper (Jack Rollins & Charles Joffe Productions, 1973)

Star Wars series (20th Century Fox, 1977 to present)

Close Encounters of the Third Kind (Columbia, 1977)

Star Trek series (Paramount, 1979 to present)

Time Bandits (Handmade Films, 1981)

The Hitchhiker's Guide to the Galaxy (BBC, 1981)

1984 (Umbrella-Rosenbloom-Virgin, 1984)

Brazil (Brazil Productions, 1985)

The Abyss (20th Century Fox, 1989)

Honey, I Shrunk the Kids (Walt Disney, 1989)

The Rocketeer (Walt Disney, 1991)

Jurassic Park (Universal, 1993)

Apollo 13 (Universal, 1995)

Contact (Warner, 1997)

Galaxy Quest (Dreamquest, 1999)

Mission to Mars (Universal, 2000)

Red Planet (Warner Bros., 2000)

MAGAZINES

Of science fiction:

Fantasy & Science Fiction

Analog

Isaac Asimov's Science Fiction Magazine

Marion Zimmer Bradley's Fantasy Magazine

Realms of Fantasy

Science Fiction Age

Amazing Stories

About science fiction:

Locus

Filmfax

Science Fiction Chronicle

Cinefantastique

WEBSITES

Science Fiction Resource Guide
http://sflovers.rutgers.edu/SFRG/
An excellent introduction to science fiction resources on the Web, with hundreds of links to authors, artists, movies, books, and other topics. A great place to start exploring science fiction on the Internet.

Uchronia
www.uchronia.net
A site devoted to the subject of alternate histories.

Empty World
www.emptyworld.co.uk
Dedicated to post-apocalyptic fiction.

The Moon in Science Fiction
www.bibliography.com/moon/
A listing of books about fictional journies to the Moon.

Alpha Ralpha Boulevard
www.Catch22.COM/~espana/SFAuthors/
A good source for biographical information about authors and artists.

Science Fiction and Fantasy for Children

http://libnt1.lib.uoguelph.ca/SFBib/index.htm

Intended mainly for parents and teachers, a good guide to fiction for young adults.

INDEX